INSTANT MACRAMÉ

TABLE OF CONTENTS

PONCHO (FRONT COVER) see Page 77 for Instructions.
VEST (BACK COVER) see Page 83 for Instructions.

Both made from "Aunt Lydia's" Heavy Rug Yarn product of
AMERICAN THREAD CO.

INTRODUCTION

"Macramé" is an Arabic word meaning ornamental fringes, braids, medallions, squares and strips. It is an old art (dating at least back to the 14th Century) that was barely kept alive in Monasteries and the Slavic Countries. About 100 years ago it was revived. Being so simple to do, it gained in popularity. Sailors in particular enjoyed making belts, bags and bell cords. Then with the introduction of radio, the hobby waned once again. However, with the present day Renaissance in arts and crafts, Macramé is rapidly becoming one of the most popular of the crafts.

We have not attempted to give you all the knots and combinations available in Macramé—this would take volumes, but we do give the most used basic knots from which you can create your own combinations.

No special talent, training or materials are needed to enjoy Macramé. It lends itself to wearing apparel, items for the home and even for wall hangings and sculptures. Once you have learned the basic Square Knot and Clove Hitch, you are ready to create your own designs. The designs in this book will give you the practice needed to master the two knots that form the foundation for Macramé. Although names of the knots and methods differ from book to book, the basic knots remain the same. Macramé is like eating peanuts—try one and you will want to make more.

"Aunt Lydia's" Heavy Rug Yarn is a product of AMERICAN THREAD CO.

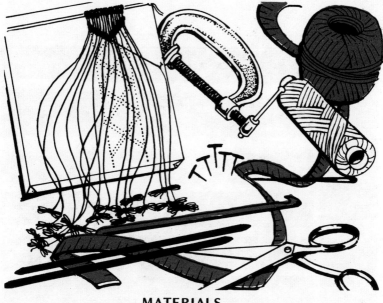

MATERIALS. . .

Cords or twines of cotton, jute, linen, sisal or nylon can be found at Hardware, Variety, Stationery, Marine or Upholstery stores. Rug yarns of cotton-and-rayon combination, wool or synthetics can be bought in Yarn Stores, Craft Shops and by Mail Order. Braids, Rattail and Rayon Cording are available at Notion Counters.

Always use materials that are firmly twisted and strong enough to take the tug and tension due to knotting.

A work board can be a pillow, tailors' ham or just a piece of heavy corrugated board, Celatex (insulating board) or cork board.

T-pins (or other sturdy pins), a pair of scissors, a ruler or tape measure and a crochet hook are also needed.

We have chosen to use "Aunt Lydia's" Heavy Rug Yarn for many of our pieces since it is easily available in a wide range of colors and it has the strength and evenness for knotting.

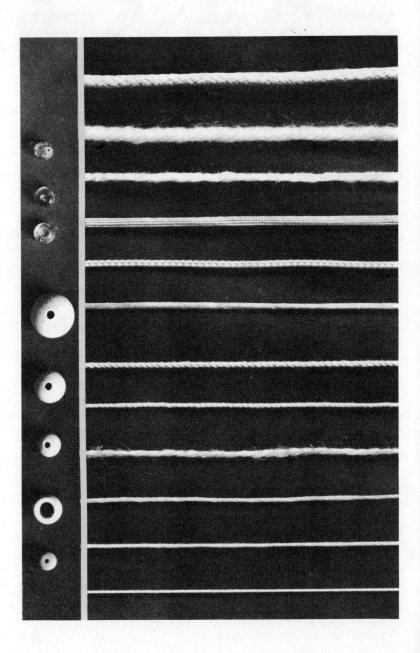

WHAT YOU SHOULD KNOW BEFORE YOU START.

Avoid yarns with elasticity since it is too difficult to keep even tension. Springy, sleek or slippery yarns may not hold the knot and present problems. If you do use a yarn that slips, apply a tiny bit of Sobo glue to the back of the knot to hold it in place.

Cords size 15 and 18 and heavier are most often used.

In general, thick cord takes more length in knotting than thin cord.

To estimate the amount of yarn needed for a design, allow between 3½ to 4 times the finished length. Then multipy by 2 since each strand is mounted with a Lark's Head. If you should run short, and this often happens, we tell you how to splice or add strands on page 51.

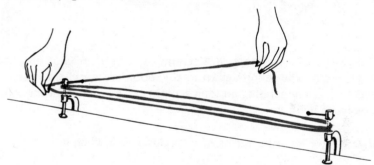

Attach C-Clamps to a table the distance apart needed to measure each length of yarn. If the length needed is too long for the table, wind the yarn from clamp to clamp as many times as needed to obtain the total length, ie: Place clamps 3' apart. Wind 3 times for a 6 yard length.

A dowel may be used in place of cord or yarn as a horizontal Knot Bearer. This is particularly successful when making a wall hanging. It not alone stabilizes the shape, but is decorative as well. I have seen reeds and dry grasses used for texture effects in wall hangings. A heavy leather strap with holes punched along the edge makes another firm mount. We used them to mount our Sling Bag on page 93.

Decorative headings can be made in numerous ways. The loop ends can be pinned and knotted as shown, then the ends horizontally Clove Hitched to a Knot Bearer cord or dowel.

To make a bobbin, wrap the cord from the middle to the end and fasten with a rubber band. In that way you can slip out cord as you need it without undoing the rubber band.

There are 2 basic knots in Macramé—the Square Knot and the Clove Hitch. The sennits given in this book are excellent practice pieces which, depending on their length, can be used as headbands, chokers or belts.

Always have Knot Bearer or Anchor Cords taut when in use.

Do not allow strands to become twisted when knotting or knots will not be uniform and attractive.

If you run short, you may be able to switch the Knot Bearer and Working Strand to finish the piece without adding another strand.

Generally you can work with as many strands as you wish, provided you use multiples of 4 strands (8, 12, 16, etc.)

Burn ends of nylon strands and add a touch of glue to ends of cotton, silk and linen strands to prevent fraying.

LARK'S HEAD

The Lark's Head (also called Reverse Double Half Hitch) is the knot most often used for attaching strands to a Knot Bearer, piece of leather, crochet, knitting or ring to start a piece. There are 2 kinds of Lark's Head knots—the Lark's Head, which gives a small bead line at the top of the work, and the Reverse Lark's Head, which gives more the appearance of a line of Clove Hitch knots at the top. The difference comes from whether you make your knot with the loop facing up or down. Both are equally easy to do—simply—

LARK'S HEAD

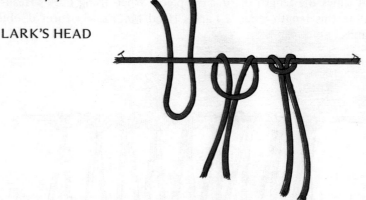

1. Fold cord in half and pass loop under Knot Bearer.

2. Pull ends through loop.

3. Draw ends tight to form knot.

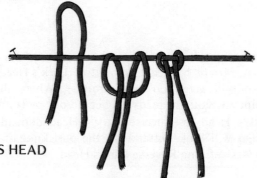

REVERSE LARK'S HEAD

MOUNTING WITH THE LARK'S HEAD

The Knot Bearer for Lark's Heads may be cord, the same yarn or braid you will be doing your piece in, or something firmer such as a dowel, knitting needle or even a glass mixing rod. The firm Knot Bearers may be removed when no longer needed resulting in a loop. However, if you are making a wall hanging, the dowel Knot Bearer may add to the design and remain as part of it.

To determine the length of working strands, measure strands 3½ to 4 times the length of finished piece. When using Lark's Heads, double this length since a Lark's Head Mount will form double strands.

First decide how many strands you need for your design at this point. Mount half that amount of Lark's Heads (since each Lark's Head will give you two strands). When all Lark's Heads are mounted, you are ready to begin your piece. Whether you use the Lark's Head or Reverse Lark's Head depends on whether your design will look better with the purl knot of the Lark's Head or the less defining Reverse Lark's Head.

OVERHAND WRAP KNOTS

The single Overhand Wrap Knot is the simple knot we have all made from childhood. The length of the wrap depends on how many times you wind the knotting strand. Overhand Wrap Knots are often used to finish ends or add decorative textures to strands.

1. Make a simple knot as illustrated. Tighten.

2. Make a simple knot but wind one end around the other three times. Pull both ends and loops will slip in line. This will give you a three-wrap knot.

3. Make a simple knot but wind one end around the other 6 times. Pull ends so loops will slip in line forming the longer wrap knot illustrated.

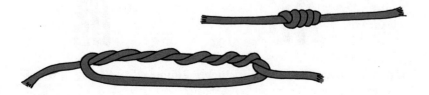

WRAPPING A COIL

What can I do with all those loose ends? Why not wrap them into a neat bunch with a tassel look. Here's how. . .

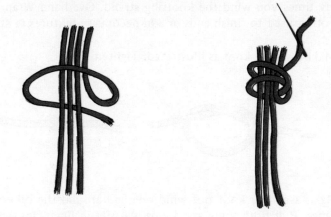

1. Wrap one cord around group of strands, overlapping first wrap as shown.

2. Continue to wrap from bottom up. Thread wrapping end on a Needlepoint Rug needle.

3. Insert needle under coils as shown. Pull needle with end through loops. Tighten.

THE CLOVE HITCH

The Clove Hitch (sometimes called the Double Half Hitch) is one of the most versatile knots. It can be used horizontally, vertically, diagonally, to form diamonds, squares and even circles (on a round item). The Clove Hitch consists of two Half Hitch Knots.

The Half Hitch is often used for sennits or increasing the distance between Clove Hitch Knots. Do a number of Half Hitch Knots along a Knot Bearer and you will find a natural twist occurring as you work. The illustration below shows you how simple the Half Hitch Knot really is.

HORIZONTAL CLOVE HITCH

1. Pin strand 1 horizontally over all the strands you wish to knot. Be sure strand 1 is taut.

2. Make a Half Hitch Knot with strand 2 as shown in illustration 2. Tighten.

3. Make the 2nd Half of the Clove Hitch Knot as shown in illustration 3.

4. Tighten. The Horizontal Clove Hitch Knot should be able to slide back and forth on strand 1. Now, continue to Clove Hitch strand 3 on strand 1, then strand 4 on strand 1, etc.

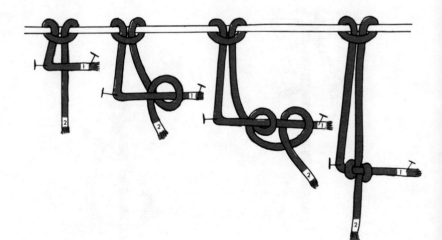

5. Clove Hitch across entire row.

6. For 2nd row pin strand 1 taut across all vertical strands. Clove Hitch back across row starting with last strand Clove Hitched on 1st row and ending with strand 2.

7. You may continue to work back and forth across piece for a close, filled-in stitch. Instead of using strand 1 as your Knot Bearer, you may choose to add a new strand to act as Knot Bearer, but you will then have to decide whether you will weave the ends into the back of your piece or use some other decorative method of finishing.

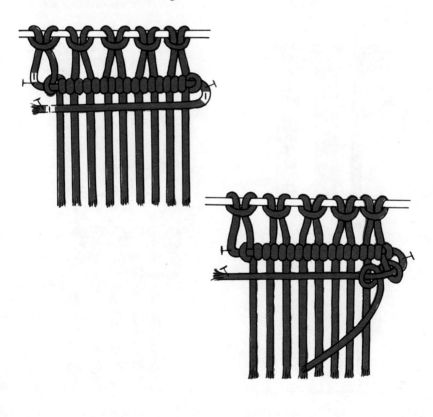

VERTICAL CLOVE HITCH
LEFT TO RIGHT

1. Pin strand 2 taut to bottom of board. Place strand 1 under strand 2.

2. Make a Half Hitch Knot as shown in illustration 2. Tighten.

3. Make the 2nd half of the Clove Hitch Knot as shown in illustration 3.

4. Tighten. The Vertical Clove Hitch Knot should be able to slide up and down on strand 2. Clove Hitch strand 1 on strand 3, then on strand 4 and all across the row. Tighten. All Clove Hitch Knots should be able to slip up and down on their Knot Bearer.

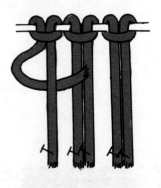

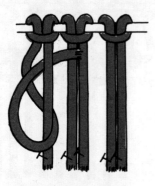

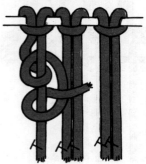

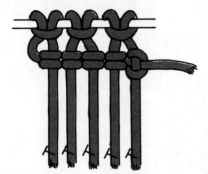

VERTICAL CLOVE HITCH—(2nd ROW)
RIGHT TO LEFT

Following illustrations 1, 2, 3, and 4, make your 2nd row of Clove Hitch Knots from right to left across the row.

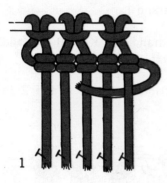

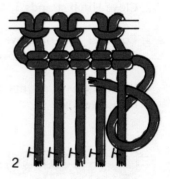

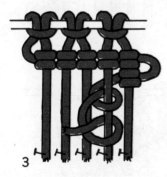

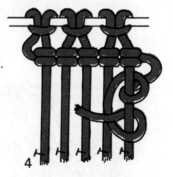

DIAGONAL CLOVE HITCH—
LEFT TO RIGHT

1. Pin strand 1 (Knot Bearer), taut, diagonally over strands to be knotted. Clove Hitch strand 2 on strand 1. (Wind strand 2 around Knot Bearer—Repeat. The 2nd wrap locks the knot. Pull knot snug.)

2. Clove Hitch strands 3, 4, etc. over strand 1.

3. For 2nd row of Clove Hitch—use strand 2 as Knot Bearer and Clove Hitch strand 3 over Knot Bearer.

4. Proceed in same manner as described in steps 1 and 2 to complete row.

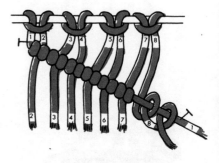

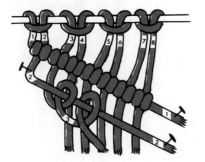
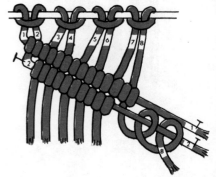

DIAGONAL CLOVE HITCH—
RIGHT TO LEFT

1. Pin strand 8 (Knot Bearer), taut, diagonally over strands to be knotted.

2. Clove Hitch strands 7, 6, 5, 4, 3, 2 and 1 over strand 8 in that order.

3. For 2nd row of Clove Hitch—Use strand 7 as Knot Bearer and Clove Hitch strand 6 over Knot Bearer.

4. Clove Hitch strand 5 over Knot Bearer (strand 7). Continue to complete row.

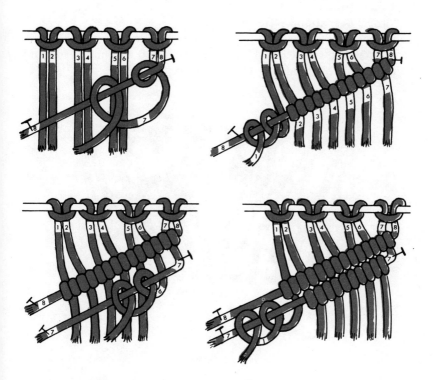

INVERTED V

Work right to left on strands 1 to 8 and left to right on strands 9 to 16. ie:

1. Pin strand 8 diagonally over strands 7 through 1.

2. Clove Hitch strands 7, 6, 5, 4, 3, 2 and 1 on strand 8 (Knot Bearer) in that order.

3. For 2nd row of Clove Hitch, use strand 7 as Knot Bearer and Clove Hitch strands 6, 5, 4, 3, 2, 1 and 8 on strand 7 (Knot Bearer) in that order.

4. Pin strand 9 diagonally over strands 10 through 16.

5. Clove Hitch strands 10, 11, 12, 13, 14, 15 and 16 (in that order) over strand 9 (Knot Bearer).

6. For 2nd row of Clove Hitch—use strand 10 as Knot Bearer and Clove Hitch strands 11, 12, 13, 14, 15, 16 and 9.

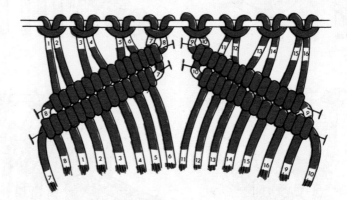

INVERTED V WITH JOINED V

1. Work a complete Inverted V.

2. Pin strand 7 diagonally from left to right over strands 8 and 1 through 6. Clove Hitch strands 8 and 1 through 6 on strand 7 in that order.

3. For the 2nd row of Clove Hitch—use strand 7 as Knot Bearer and Clove Hitch strands 8 and 1 through 6 on strand 7 in that order.

4. Pin strand 10 diagonally from right to left over strands 9 and 16 through 11. Clove Hitch strands 9 and 16 through 11 over strand 10, in that order.

5. Place strand 10 together with strands 1 through 8 and strand 7 together with strands 9 through 16.

6. For 2nd row of Clove Hitch—use strand 9 as Knot Bearer and Clove Hitch strands 16 through 11 and 7, on strand 9, in that order. Using strand 8 as Knot Bearer, Clove Hitch strands 1 through 6 and 10 and 9 on strand 8.

OPEN V

Clove Hitch strand 1 on strand 2 (Knot Bearer). Clove Hitch strand 16 on strand 15 (Knot Bearer).

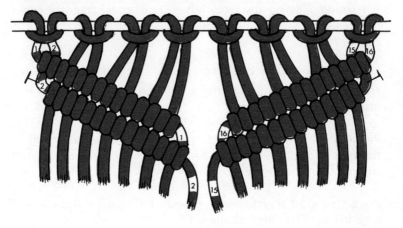

JOINED V

Cross strands 1 and 2 (Knot Bearers) over strands 9 through 15. Clove Hitch strand 16 on strand 1 (Knot Bearer) then Clove Hitch strand 15 on strand 2.

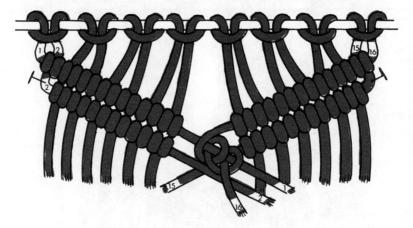

THE SQUARE KNOT

The Square Knot consists of 2 half knots. When worked continuously, you cannot readily recognize the Left Square Knot from the Right Square Knot. But when worked individually, the direction becomes apparent as illustrated.

illus. Left Square Knot/Right Square Knot

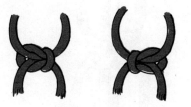

Therefore we have broken the Square Knot into 4 parts. There are also 2 methods of making Square Knots. Method 1 is comprised of 2 steps (1st step is making the 1st half knot—2nd step is making the 2nd half knot). Method 2 works both half knots in 1 step. It is sometimes advantageous to use both methods in the same piece.

Square Knots can be made from 2 strands or multi-strands. Pgs. 27 and 29 illustrate the 2-strand knot. You may also use 2 or more strands to replace the single strand shown. By increasing the number of strands used for knotting, you will get a larger, bulkier knot.

illus. Two Strands/Multi-strands

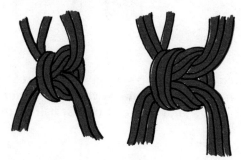

Knots on Pgs. 28 and 30 may be made over as many strands (Knot Bearers) as you wish. The more Knot Bearers, the wider and flatter the finished knot will be.

Over 2 strands

Over 4 strands

All Square Knots given in this section will be Left Square Knots. If you wish to make any of them a Right Square Knot merely make the 2nd half of the knot first and the 1st half of the knot as the 2nd step.

THE SQUARE KNOT—METHOD 1.

1. Place strand 2 over and under strand 1 and out through loop.
   Tighten.

2. Place strand 2 over and under strand 1. Place end of strand 1
   over, through loop and then under strand 2.

3. Tighten.

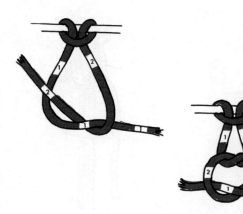

THE SQUARE KNOT OVER 2 KNOT BEARERS
—METHOD 1.

1. Place strand 1 over strands 2 and 3 (Knot Bearers). Place strand 4 over the end of strand 1, under strands 3 and 2, up through the loop and out over strand 1. Tighten.

2. Place strand 1 over strands 3 and 2. Place strand 4 over end of strand 1.

3. Bring strand 4 under strands 1, 2 and 3, up through loop and out over strand 1.

4. Tighten.

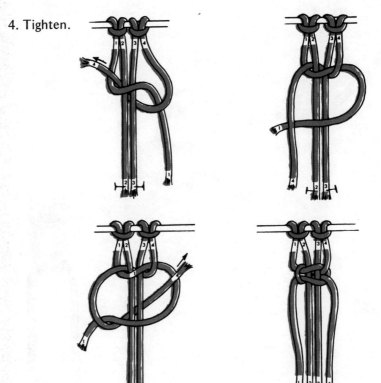

THE SQUARE KNOT—METHOD 2.

1. Holding strand 1 in the left hand, form a closed loop as shown.

2. Place part A of loop under parts B forming a pretzel as illustrated.

3. Weave strand 2 through loops starting from back to front as shown. Pull points B to the left and point A under strand 2 to the right.

4. Straighten and move knot into position. First tighten top half of knot, then lower half.

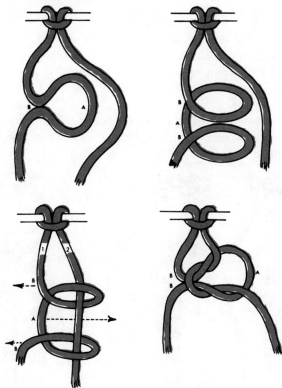

THE SQUARE KNOT OVER 2 KNOT BEARERS
—METHOD 2.

This method ties both parts of the Square Knot in one step. The trick is in pulling the right strands illustrated with A and B in step 3. Once you get this, the knot forms very easily.

1. Form a closed loop with strand 1 over strands 2 and 3 (Knot Bearers).

2. Put thumb and forefinger of right hand through loop, under Knot Bearers and grasp the other 2 parts of strand 1 at points B, bringing them back through the loop A. You now have 2 loops together.

3. Bring strand 4 down through these 2 loops. With the left hand, hold the 2 strands at point B (indicated with the arrow pointing left. With the right hand pick up the loop (A) under the Knot Bearers and pull it to the right as indicated by the arrow.

4. You can now see both parts of the Square Knot. Straighten and move knot into position. First tighten top half of knot and then lower half.

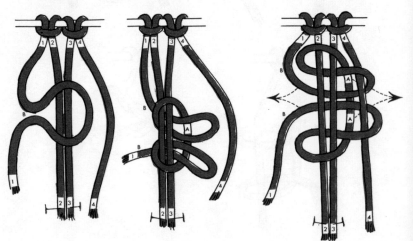

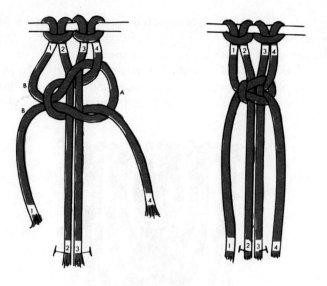

GRADED SQUARE KNOTS

The Graded Square Knot illustrated was made with 12 strands. Other variations may be made. This knot works best with firmer cords & twines.

1. Using strands 6 and 7 as Knot Bearers, make a square Knot using strands 5 and 8.

2. Using strands 5, 6, 7 and 8 as Knot Bearers, make a Square Knot using strands 4 and 9.

3. Using strands 4 thru 9 as Knot Bearers, make a Square Knot using strands 3 and 10.

4. Using strands 3 thru 10 as Knot Bearers, make a Square Knot using strands 2 and 11.

5. Using strands 2 thru 11 as Knot Bearers, make a Square Knot using strands 1 and 12. This forms a pyramid shape.

6. To form a diamond as illustrated, continue to make Square Knots over the multi-core Knot Bearers, except with each knot, omit using the working strands just used for the previous knot. ie: omit using strands 1 and 12. Using strands 3 thru 10 as Knot Bearers, make a Square Knot using strands 2 and 11. Work in this manner until only strands 6 and 7 remain as Knot Bearers.

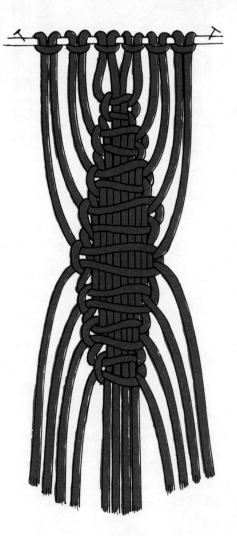

ADDITIONAL KNOTS

THE MONKEY'S FIST

Navy men are familiar with the decorative dangle knot called the Monkey's Fist since many of them have used this knot to make a weight they use to anchor their dinghy on the beach. Of course their knot was much larger, and instead of a bead, they used a rock as the core. To make this knot. . .

1. Starting with about a 1½ yard length of cord, wind cord 4 times vertically over two fingers.

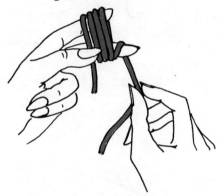

2. Bring cord between fingers and wind from back around all strands 4 times horizontally, working from bottom to top. Do not tighten.

3. Bring cord around front of horizontal winds and then through the top loop, then bottom loop. Continue to wind through these loops 4 times. Do not tighten.

4. Remove fingers and insert a bead (¼" or larger) into center.

5. Bring end of cord through bottom loop.

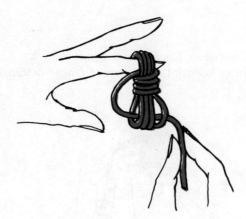

6. Tighten strands around bead by starting with one end and following that strand around the bead, tightening each loop as you go. Keep strands parallel and when possible do not allow them to cross. This is the only ticklish part of the knot, following the loops of only 1 strand and tightening them going around the bead.

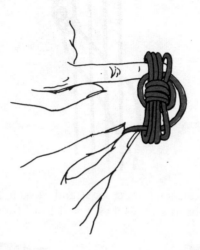

Do *not* try to tighten more than one continuous strand and work only in *one* direction.

TRIANGLE KNOT

1. Lay strand 6 diagonally across strands 1 to 5 and pin securely. Clove Hitch, using strands 5, 4, 3, 2 and 1 in that order, on strand 6.

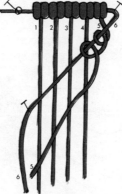

2. Lay strand 5 diagonally across strands 4 to 1 and pin securely. Clove Hitch, using strands 4, 3, 2 and 1 on strand 5.

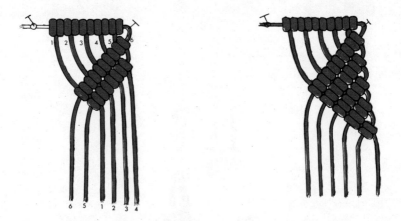

3. Clove Hitch strands 3, 2 and 1 on strand 4. Clove Hitch strands 2 and 1 on strand 3. Clove Hitch strand 2 on strand 1.

36

LEAF MOTIF (3 VARIATIONS)

LEAF 1.
1. Place strand 1 (Knot Bearer) diagonally across strands 2 to 8. Clove Hitch strands 2 to 8 on Knot Bearer, forming a gentle curve with the Knot Bearer as you knot. Using strand 2 as Knot Bearer, Clove Hitch strands 3 to 8 and 1 on Knot Bearer (2) forming a gentle curve in the opposite direction as you knot. Knot 1 from the second curve and knot 8 from the first curve should meet. This will form one leaf.

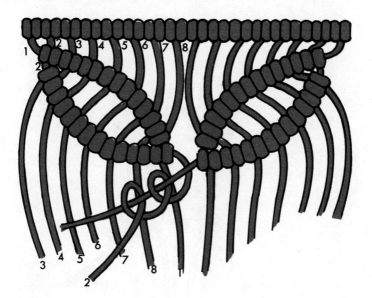

2. The leaf in the opposite direction is made by placing strand 16 diagonally across strands 15 to 9 and Clove Hitching with strands 15 to 9 on Knot Bearer (16) in that order. Form the same gentle curve as you did for the first leaf. Place strand 15 across strands 14 to 9 and 16 and Clove Hitch in that order, again forming a gentle reverse curve which will meet the top curve with the last knot.

LEAF 2.

1. Using strand 8 as Knot Bearer, Clove Hitch strands 7, 6 and 5 in that order, on strand 8. Using strand 7 as Knot Bearer, Clove Hitch strands 6, 5 and 8 on strand 7. Using strand 1 as Knot Bearer, Clove Hitch strands 2, 3 and 4 on strand 1. Using strand 2 as Knot Bearer, Clove Hitch strands 3, 4, 1, 7, 8, 5 and 6, in that order, on strand 2. Using strand 8 as Knot Bearer, Clove Hitch strands 5, 6 and 2 on strand 8. Using strand 7 as Knot Bearer, Clove Hitch strands 1, 4 and 3 on strand 7. Using strand 1 as Knot Bearer, Clove Hitch strands 4, 3, and 7, in that order, on strand 1. You have now completed a four-leaf clover motif.

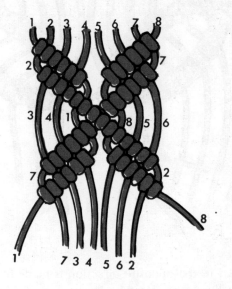

LEAF 3.

1. Using strand 8 as Knot Bearer, Clove Hitch strands 7 to 1 in that order, on strand 8, curving gently as you work. Using strand 7 as Knot Bearer, Clove Hitch strands 6 to 1 and 8 in that order, on strand 7, curving gently upward until the knots meet. To get the alternating effect of the design, use strand 4 as Knot Bearer and Clove Hitch strands 5, 6, 7, 8, etc. on strand 4. Using strand 5 as Knot Bearer, Clove Hitch strands 6, 7, 8, etc. on strand 5.

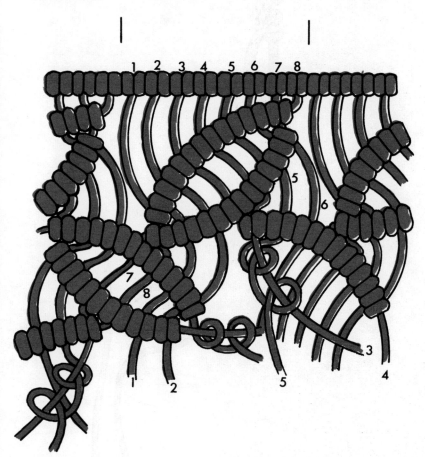

BUTTONHOLE KNOT

Use strand 1 as Knot Bearer. Using strand 2, Half Hitch continuously for entire length as shown.

CHINESE CROWN KNOT

1. With strand 1, form a reverse S.

2. With strand 2, weave under and over strand 1 as illustrated.

3. Tighten.

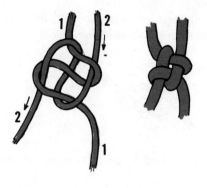

or. . .

2. With strand 2, weave under the top cord, over the next 2, back
   under all 3, over 2 and under 1 as illustrated.

3. Tighten.

The Chinese Crown Knot may be made with 2 or more strands
worked together as shown in illustration.

JOSEPHINE KNOT

1. Lay a loop of cord #1 over cord #2. Place free end of cord #2 over free end of cord #1 as shown.

2. Bring free end of cord #2 under top end of cord #1.

3. Weave free end of cord #2 over cord #1 and under cord #2 as shown. Even loops and tighten.

4. Use as many strands as you wish, but always be sure to keep strands in line and lying flat.

"GOBELIN KNOTTED WORK"—"CAVANDOLI WORK" "KNOTTED TAPESTRY"

Some articles you may wish to make may call for a close weave, such as rugs, eyeglass cases, purses, etc. Or—you may want a specific design or monogram on a piece. The technique we illustrate here, sometimes called "Knotted Tapestry", "Gobelin Knotted Work" or "Cavandoli Work", can accomplish this for you. It is made up of Horizontal and Vertical Clove Hitch Knots. The trick is where each is used.

1. Work out your design on graph paper. To determine the number of strands needed, make a small 2" X 2" swatch and count the number of strands used. This will help you in making your chart as each square should equal one knot.

We are giving you a graph of the alphabet to help you if you desire to make monograms.

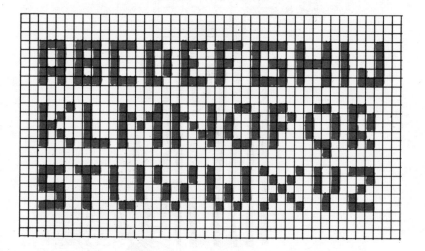

2. Cut an Anchor Cord, of color A, 4″ longer than the intended width of your piece. Pin to Work Board. Cut as many strands of A (10 times the intended length of your piece). Fold each strand in half and Lark's Head to Anchor Cord.

3. Cut a 3 or 5 yard length (depending on the bulk of the yarn) of color B.

4. Pin one end to side of Work Board. Place strand of color B across all strands of color A close to Lark's Heads. Now follow chart carefully. To show color A, make a Horizontal Clove Hitch Knot (See page 16) on Knot Bearer (color B). To show color B, make a Vertical Clove Hitch Knot (See page 18) using color A as Knot Bearer. Remember, working Knot shows color. Color of Knot Bearer disappears inside Working Knot. Now follow your chart carefully to complete design.

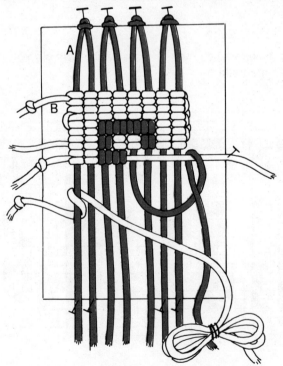

CAVANDOLI EYEGLASS CASE

MATERIALS:
1 skein "Aunt Lydia's" beige Rug Yarn; 1 skein "Aunt Lydia's"
orange Rug Yarn; Work Board; T-pins; large eye needle.

DIRECTIONS:

1. Cut a 2 foot length of beige yarn for Anchor Cord. Center and pin to Work Board; remaining ends at each side will be used later to join back to front. Cut seven 2 yard lengths of beige yarn; fold in half and Lark's Head to center of Anchor Cord.

2. Make a bobbin of a 3 yard length of orange yarn. Make a knot in loose end and pin to side of Work Board. Make a row of Vertical Clove Hitch Knots (See page 18) with orange yarn as Working Strands and beige yarn as Knot Bearers. Pin orange yarn across beige strands and Horizontal Clove Hitch (See page 16) beige strands on orange Knot Bearers.

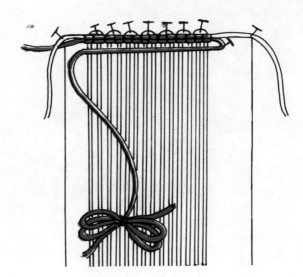

3. Continue to follow chart until entire piece is completed. Always work orange strands as Vertical Clove Hitch Knots, and beige strands as Horizontal Clove Hitch Knots.

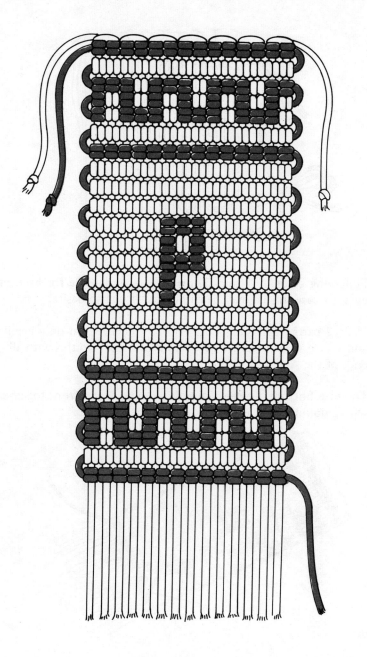

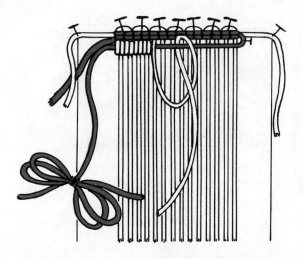

4. Following steps 1, 2 and 3, make a second piece for back of eyeglass case. Initial may be eliminated if you so desire.

5. Place 2 parts, right sides out. Thread Anchor Cord on a needle and weave sides together to bottom of piece. Do this with all 4 ends of the Anchor Cords.

6. To close bottom, tie beige strands from back and front together with a double knot. Cut fringe even at bottom.

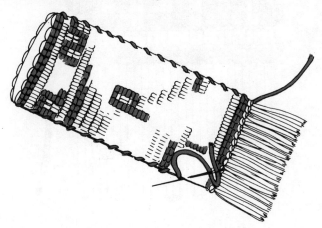

COLORING CORDS AND YARNS

"Aunt Lydia's" Heavy Rug yarn comes in a beautiful range of colors; but it is rather difficult to find cords and twine in pretty colors. However, you can dye most cords by following the directions on the dye package. It is better to dye the cords before tying. To prevent tangling, wind the cords in loose skeins and carefully place in the dye solution. If you can't boil the dye, add a cup of vinegar to each package of dye to help set the color. Try to dye all the material needed at one time to get a uniform color.

ADDING BEADS, ETC.

The hardest part is finding beads with large enough holes. If you can't find any, you can make them from self hardening clay, either left in the natural color, or rubbed with the metallic wax finishes sold in the craft stores for a metallic look. Or—you may use papier maché and paint them or cut triangles of gift-wrap paper and roll and glue them into cylindrical beads. To thread them on a cord or string, dip the ends of the cords into melted wax and form a point or attach a short fine wire to the end. You may find a Steel Crochet Hook #0 helpful in pulling soft yarn through the bead's hole as illustrated. But don't stop at beads—shells, bells, rings, buttons and feathers make other fine additions to your pieces.

*To work circular: Do not fold strands in half; instead tie firmly in the center. Clove Hitch a plastic or metal ring to get strands radiating like spokes from the center as illustrated.

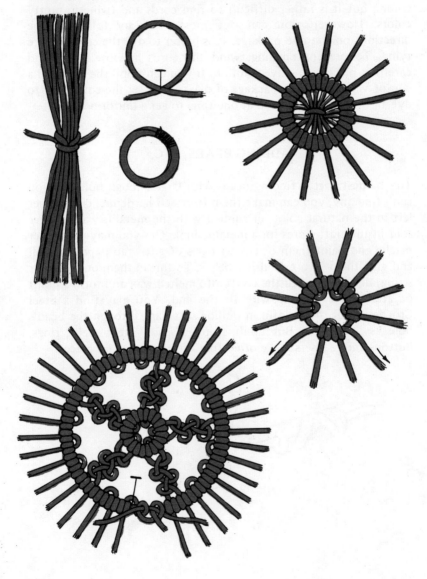

*Adding a double strand: Pin loop end of new strand in position between strands of piece. Knot each new strand into the piece as if it were already part of it.

*A new Knot Bearer cord may be added for making Clove Hitch Knots. The ends of the Knot Bearer can be woven into the under side of the piece when it is finished.

*Running Short: If you have underestimated the length of a strand you can add another strand. If you find yourself short when working Clove Hitch Knots, overlap ends as illustrated and continue knotting the row. If you run short when making Square Knots, overlap ends as illustrated and continue knotting. If more than 1 strand must be added, stagger the overlapping to avoid lumps in the finished piece.

*Splicing: Ends may be spliced together by untwisting the cords. Overlap the opened ends, twist together one at a time, glue each to hold. Now twist all strands together to match twist of cord as close as possible and glue.

Macramé can be made more interesting by the use of 2 or more colors combined in one piece. However, this does call for a bit more planning. One color can be carried invisibly to another part of the piece by using it as a Knot Bearer. As a Knot Bearer it is covered by the working strands. To make it appear, use it as your Working Strands.

Or—you may add strands of a 2nd color by pinning the center of the strand in position and knotting it into the design as if it had always been part of the piece.

By using the Straddle Lark's Head (see page 53), you can control color in Sennits.

Just remember—
  Show a color with Working Strands.
  Hide a color with Knot Bearers.

What to do with the ends of strands when the piece is finished:

1. You can cut the ends even—knot the tips and allow to remain as fringe.

2. You can group and knot them and trim evenly as tassels.

3. You can knot beads to the tips for a weighted fringe.

4. You can (with a crochet hook) weave the ends back into the piece and cut away the excess and glue ends to hold.

5. You can end a piece with 2 or more rows of horizontal Clove Hitching and weave the tips back into the Clove Hitch Knots.

6. In the case of a rug you may prefer to machine stitch rug tape around the edge. Turn the tape under and slip-stitch the tape to the back of the rug as shown.

SENNITS OR BRAIDS

Usually 4 strands are used—2 Working Strands and 2 Knot Bearers. However, in Sennit 6 we have worked all 4 strands.

It should be remembered that the Knot Bearers take about ⅓ to ¼ the amount of yarn that the Working Strands do—so measure accordingly.

You may have 2 Lark's Heads next to one another or make one Lark's Head straddling a center one as we have done below. You may like to try this when working with 2 colors.

The bottom of each Sennit illustrates how the knot for that particular one was made. The Sennit on this page were made only of Square Knots.

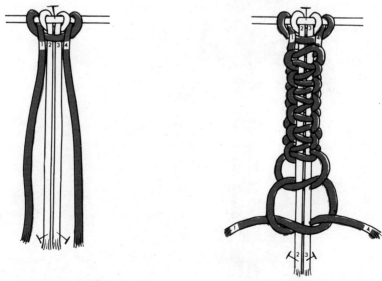

STRADDLE LARK'S HEAD   SENNIT 1

SENNIT 2 was made by using only one-half of the Square Knot. Part 1 of the Square Knot will make the Sennit twist in one direction, while part 2 of the Square Knot will make it twist in the reverse.

SENNIT 3 was made by Clove Hitching strand 1 first on strand 2 and then
on strands 2 and 3. Then strand 4 was
Clove Hitched on strand 3 and then
on strands 3 and 4.

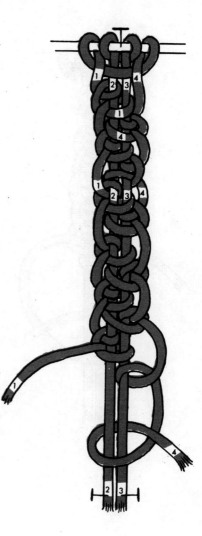

SENNIT 4 alternates Clove Hitching strand 1 on strands 2 and 3 and then Clove Hitching strand 4 on strands 3 and 2.

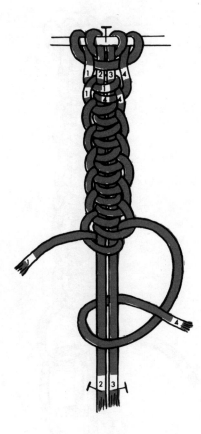

SENNIT 5 uses only the Square Knot plus a few tricky (but easy) twists to get the effect. In this Sennit, strands 1 and 4 are crossed and strands 2 and 3 (Knot Bearers) are then laid over the ends giving the effect of weaving.

SENNIT 6 alternates Working Strands and Knot Bearers. First strands 1 and 4 are Square Knotted over strands 2 and 3. Then strands 2 and 3 are Square Knotted over strands 1 and 4.

SENNIT 7 shows knots resulting in open and closed work. First, strand 1 is Clove Hitched on strand 2 and strand 4 is Clove Hitched on strand 3. Then Barrel Beads are threaded on strands 2 and 3. Again strand 1 is Clove Hitched on strand 2 and strand 4 is Clove Hitched on strand 3. Now make a Square Knot working strands 1 and 4 over Knot Bearer strands 2 and 3. Repeat as many times as desired.

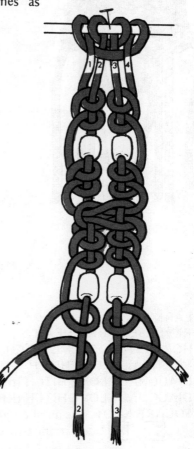

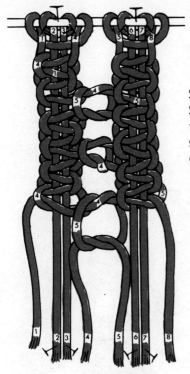

SENNIT 8 is made up of 2 Sennits of Square Knots joined every 2nd Knot with a Square Knot made with the strands from each Sennit closest to each other.

SYMBOLS

LARK'S HEAD	∩
REVERSE LARK'S HEAD	U
HORIZONTAL CLOVE HITCH	
VERTICAL CLOVE HITCH	
DIAGONAL CLOVE HITCH (right to left)	
DIAGONAL CLOVE HITCH (left to right)	

SQUARE KNOT (the numbers inside squares indicate the number
2   4   of strands to be used for each Square Knot).

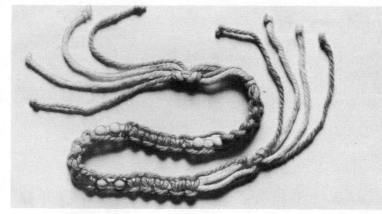

HEADBAND AND CHOKER

This is the quickest and simplest item you can make. An excellent and rewarding piece for the beginner.

MATERIALS:
2 yard length of pink "Aunt Lydia's" Heavy Rug Yarn; 7 yard length of rose "Aunt Lydia's" Heavy Rug Yarn; 6 small wooden beads with large holes, Size 0 steel crochet hook; Work Board (approx. 9" X 12"), tape measure, T-pins.

3

DIRECTIONS:

1. Cut 1 pink strand 2 yards long (for Knot Bearer) and 1 rose strand 7 yards long for Working Strand. Fold in half and pin fold end to Work Board as shown in Detail 1.

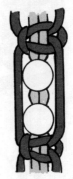

1

2. 6" from fold edge make a Square Knot (Detail 2).

3. Make a 5-knot Square Knot Sennit (Detail 3). See page 61

2

4. String 2 small wooden beads on 2 pink strands as shown in Detail 4.

5. Repeat steps 3 and 4 two more times.

6. Repeat step 3 once more

7. 2" from Sennit, make a Square. Knot as in step 2. Leave 6" of strands free.

8. Make an Overhand Knot at the end of each strand. Trim off excess.

4

BELT A

This belt has a sturdy, yet feminine appearance. It is very simple to make since it consists of the Triangle Knot reversed and repeated as many times as you wish for desired length.

MATERIALS:
Approximately 60 yds. of Rattail (tubular satin), 24 amber Pony beads, T-pins, Work Board (approx. 9" X 12"), rubber bands, tracing paper, pencil.

DIRECTIONS:
Make tracing of chart. Pin chart to Work Board.

1. To determine length of strands, multiply your waist measure by 4, and add 1 yard for fringe. Cut 12 strands this length and pin to board 14" from edge of strands (for fringe). Roll loose ends into wads held in place with rubber bands.

2. 14" from ends of strands, make a Square Knot of strands 1, 2, 3 and 10, 11, 12 over Knot Bearers (strands 4-9). Using these same strands make a half of a Square Knot.

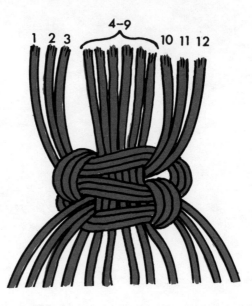

3. 1" from 1½ Square Knot, make a Square Knot of strands 6 and 7 (See page 25).

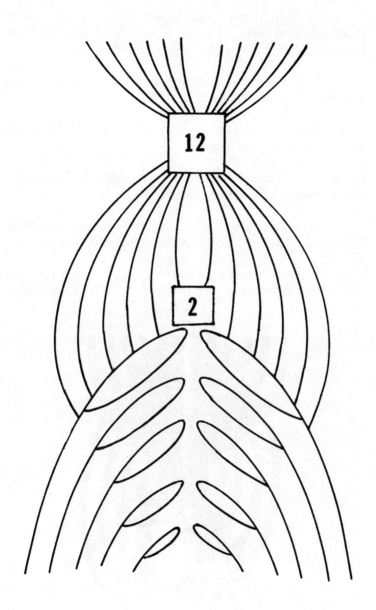

4. Pin strand 7 diagonally (right to left, following direction on chart) across strands 5-1, (this is your Knot Bearer). Clove Hitch strands 5, 4, 3, 2 and 1 (in that order) on strand 7.

5. Pin strand 5 diagonally across strands 4-1. Clove Hitch strands 4-1 on Knot Bearer (strand 5).

6. Pin strand 4 diagonally across strands 3-1. Clove Hitch strands 3-1 on Knot Bearer (strand 4).

7. Pin strand 3 diagonally across strands 2 and 1. Clove Hitch strands 2 and 1 on Knot bearer (strand 3).

8. Pin strand 2 over strand 1. Clove Hitch strand 1 on Knot Bearer (strand 2). You have now completed one Triangle.

9. Make a Reverse Triangle by pinning strand 6 (left to right) over strands 8-12. Clove Hitch strands 8-12 on Knot Bearer (strand 6).

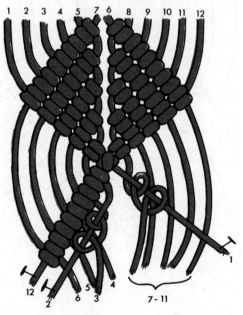

10. Pin strand 8 diagonally over strands 9-12. Clove Hitch strands 9-12 over Knot Bearer (strand 8).

11. Pin strand 9 diagonally over strands 10-12. Clove Hitch strands 10-12 on Knot Bearer (strand 9).

12. Pin strand 10 diagonally over strands 11 and 12. Clove Hitch strands 11 and 12 on Knot Bearer (strand 10).

13. Pin strand 11 over strand 2. Clove Hitch strand 12 on Knot Bearer (strand 11). Make a Square Knot of center strands 6 and 7. You have now completed your Reverse Triangle and one whole unit of your belt.

14. Repeat steps 4 through 13 as many times as necessary to obtain waist measure (we made our belt of 28 units).

15. Repeat 1½ Square Knot (described in step 2) 1″ below last unit.

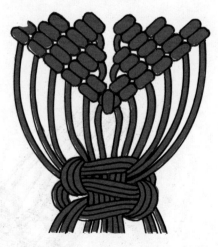

16. Cut strands at each end of belt same length. String 1 Pony Bead and make an Overhand Knot at end of each strand. Cut off excess.

BELTS WITH BUCKLES

Making a belt with a buckle is no problem—simply start your belt by making your Lark's Heads on the cross-bar of the buckle. Be sure to have the same amount of strands each side of the prong (if there is one). The spaces between strands act as eyelets to put the prong through at the other end of your belt.

One of the most popular forms of macrame that sailors did was belts made in two colors. They worked their name or monogram and sometimes a date in the Cavandoli Knot. This made a strong, attractive belt.

You may wish to use a floral, butterfly, bird or abstract design for your Cavandoli belt. However, many other knots work equally well. The Leaf Knot, or Clove Hitch diamonds or triangles make a beautiful, unusual belt. Use your imagination and combine different knots to create your one-of-a-kind designs.

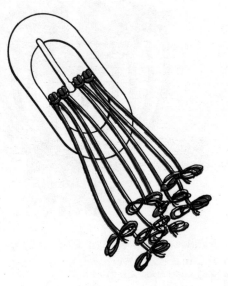

BELT B

This sturdy Seine Cord belt can be made to blend with any color costume by picking up the colors in the beads used in the fringe. This is an easy and rewarding belt to make.

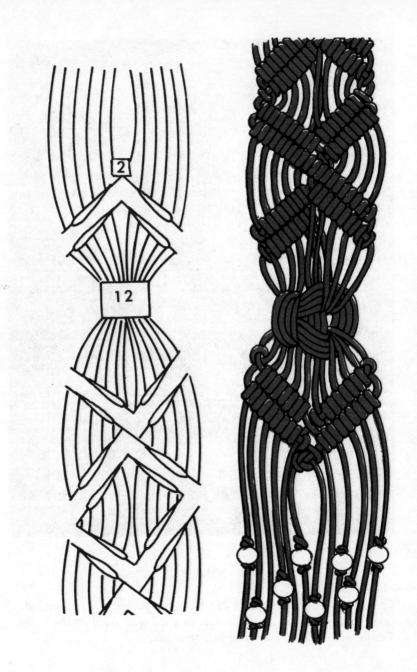

MATERIALS:
60 yards Seine Cord, 12 Amethyst glass beads, 12 turquoise glass beads, Work Board (9″ X 12″), T-Pins, scissors, rubber bands.

DIRECTIONS:
Cut 12 strands 4½ yards each. Trace chart and pin to Work Board. Pin Strands 18″ from ends. Follow chart carefully for placing of knots (indicated by symbols).

1. Make a Square Knot (see pg. 27) with strands 6 and 7.

2. Pin strand 6 (Knot Bearer) from right to left over strands 5-1, following lines on chart. Clove Hitch strands 5-1 on Knot Bearer.

3. Pin strand 7 (Knot Bearer) left to right over strands 8-12 following lines on chart. Clove Hitch strands 7-12 on Knot Bearer.

4. Work a 2nd row of Clove Hitches to correspond.

5. Make a ⬚12 Square Knot using strands 1-4 and 9-12 on Knot Bearing strands 5-8 in position shown on chart.

6. Pin strand 1 (Knot Bearer) diagonally left to right over strands 2-6. Clove Hitch strands 2-6 on Knot Bearer.

7. Pin strand 12 (Knot Bearer) diagonally right to left over strands 11-7. Clove Hitch strands 11-7 on Knot Bearer in that order.

8. Pin strand 11 (Knot Bearer) diagonally right to left over next 5 strands. Clove Hitch all 5 strands on Knot Bearer.

9. Pin strand 2 diagonally left to right over next 11 strands. Clove Hitch all strands on Knot Bearer.

10. Repeat Step 2.

11. Repeat Step 3.

12. Pin strand 5 (Knot Bearer) diagonally right to left over next 5 strands. Clove Hitch all 5 strands on Knot Bearer.

13. Repeat Steps 6, 7, 8, 9, 10, 11 and 12 twelve times, ending with Step 5, 2 Clove Hitch rows and Step 1.

14. String 1 bead on each strand—push to random height, alternating colors. Make a Knot each side of bead and at end of each strand.

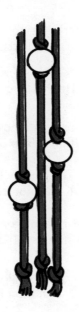

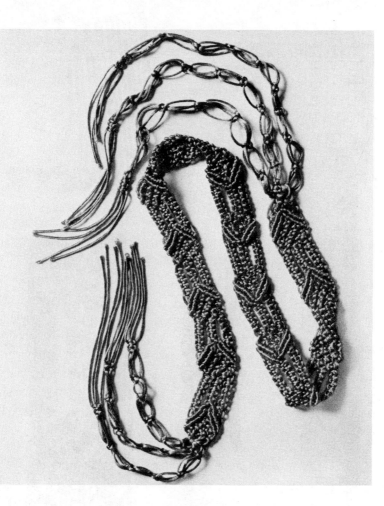

BELT C

This belt is made of tubular rayon-satin cord (known as Rattail) which is ¹⁄₁₆″ thick; any similar cord can be used. Original belt is about 1½″ wide and 33″ long without fringe. For a shorter or longer belt, omit or add desired number of rows at each end, but always end with a Square Knot made with all 12 strands. For easier handling belt is worked from the center (see Chart).

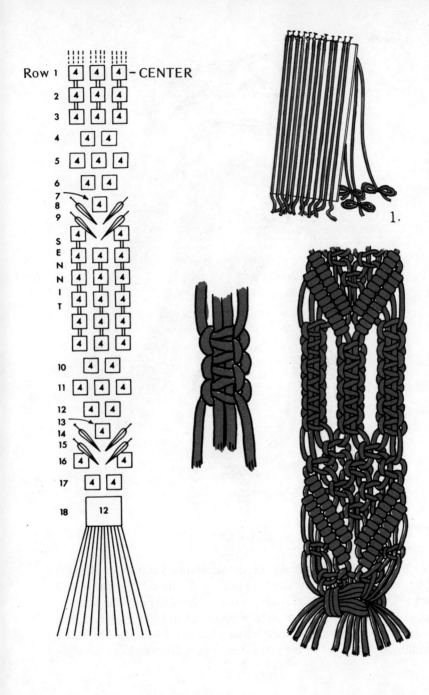

Row 1 [4] [4] [4] — CENTER
2 [4] [4] [4]
3 [4] [4] [4]
4 [4] [4]
5 [4] [4] [4]
6 [4] [4]
7 [4]
8
9

S
E
N [4]   [4]
N [4]   [4]
I [4]   [4]
T [4]   [4]
   [4]   [4]
   [4]   [4]

10 [4] [4]
11 [4] [4] [4]
12 [4] [4]
13 [4]
14
15
16 [4]   [4]

17 [4] [4]

18 [12]

1.

74

MATERIALS:

55 yds. Rattail, scotch tape, Work Board, T-Pins, scissors

NOTE: If making belt of different material than given above, width will vary; also yardage will vary from amount given above. If longer or shorter belt is desired (see directions above). To determine the length of strands, multiply your waist measure by 4. Cut 12 strands this length plus 30" for fringe. Fold each strand in half to find center; pin center of each strand (strands 1-12) to Work Board (see Detail 1). Knot the loose strands together above pins; place them over top of board and scotch-tape them securely to back.

Row 1: Starting at center of belt and FIRST ROW on CHART, divide the 12 strands into 3 groups of 4; working from left to right work 3 Square Knots with 4 strands (see page 27); this will be the beginning of 3 Square Knot Sennits (see page 53).

Rows 2 and 3: Complete each Sennit with 2 more 4 Square Knots, placing them below each other. Follow chart carefully for placement of Knots.

Row 4: Skip first and last 2 strands, 2 Square Knot groups of 4 strands each.

Row 5: 3 Square Knot groups of 4 strands each.

Row 6: Repeat 4th row.

Row 7: Skip first and last 4 strands, 1 Square Knot over 4 center strands.

Row 8: Work a Left to Right Diagonal Clove Hitch with strands 1-6 using strand 1 as Knot Bearer (see page 20) and Right to Left Diagonal Clove Hitch with strands 7-12 using strand 12 as Knot Bearer (see page 21).

Row 9: Work in same manner as 8th row using strands 2 and 11 as Knot Bearers.

Work a Square Knot Sennit of 6 Square Knots over strands 1, 2, 3, 4 and 9, 10, 11, 12 and another Sennit of 5 Square Knots over strands 5, 6, 7, and 8.

Repeat Rows 4 through 9 and Sennits 5 times, end with last 9 rows (see chart). Work a 4 Square Knot with strands 1, 2, 3 & 4 and another with strands 9, 10, 11 & 12. In the next row make a Square Knot of strands 3, 4, 5 & 6 and another of strands 7, 8, 9 & 10, end with a 12 Square Knot (4 left and 4 right over center 4 strands).

FRINGE: Divide the 12 strands into 3 groups of 4 each and work one 4 Square Knot below 12 Square Knot and 7 more 4 Square Knots 1 inch apart (see Detail 2) ending with Sennit of 3 Square Knots. Work other 2 groups in same manner. Trim ends evenly. This completes half of belt. Remove work from Work Board, turn your work around and pin 1st Row of finished part (same side up as before) to Work Board.

Work other half in same manner following Chart from 1st Row to end.

2

MACRAMÉ PONCHO

Poncho was designed in one piece and fits from size 10 to 16. It was made with "Aunt Lydia's" Heavy Rug Yarn and wooden Barrel Beads of several colors. The neckline is adjustable, looks especially nice with pants, but would be a knockout at the beach over beach wear.

MATERIALS:
7-70 yd. skeins "Aunt Lydia's" Heavy Rug Yarn
84 Magenta, 42 Rose & 42 Pink wooden barrel shaped beads,
T-Pins, scissors, muslin 36" X 36", Work Board 36" X 36", Steel
Crochet Hook #0 for pulling yarn through beads

DIRECTIONS:
1. Enlarge graph. Mark center on muslin. Draw circles 5", 9" and
   12" from center. Place on Work Board.

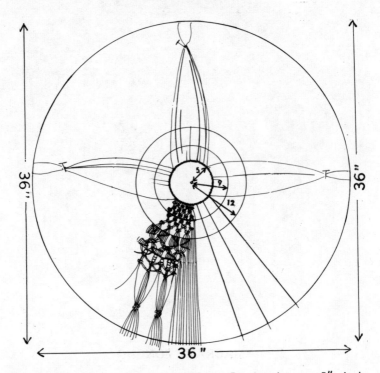

2. Cut 2 Knot Bearers each 2 yds long. Pin in place to 5" circle.

3. Cut 84 (2½ yd.) strands. Fold each strand in half and knot
   over Knot Bearers with Lark's Heads (see detail on pg.11 for
   Lark's Head knot). Pin strands in place on muslin covered
   Work Board.

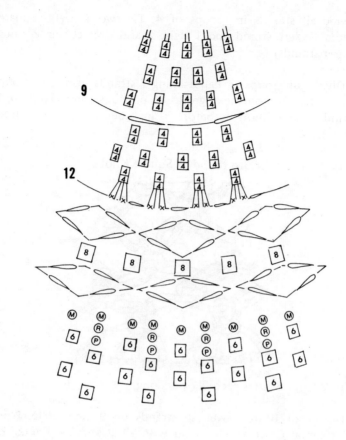

4. Divide all strands in groups of 4. Tie two 4 strand Square Knots (1 left strand and 1 right strand over center 2 Knot Bearer strands).

5. * Divide all groups in half (taking 2 strands from one group and 2 strands from next group of previous row). Tie two 4 strand Square Knots as before ½ inch below first group (see Chart).

6. Repeat from * for 3rd round of Square Knots.

7. Cut 2 Knot Bearers each 2¼ yds. long.

8. Place Knot Bearers over all strands on 9 inch circle. Work Horizontal Clove Hitch round with all strands (see detail on page 16 for Horizontal Clove Hitch).

9. Work 3 alternating rounds of two 4 strand Square Knots as before.

10. Cut 2 Knot Bearers each 2½ yds. long. Place over all strands on 12" line. Clove Hitch all strands same as before.

11. Cut 42 strands each 2 yds. long. Fold strands in half. Attach 1 folded strand between strands 1 and 2 and 1 folded strand between strands 3 and 4 of each 4 strand group with Reverse

Lark's Head Knot (see detail on page 11 for Reverse Lark's Head Knot). Each of the 42 groups now has 8 strands.

12. Pin strand 1 from left to right diagonally over 7 strands. Work 7 Clove Hitches over strand 1. Pin same strand 1 from right to left diagonally over 7 strands. Work 7 Clove Hitches over strand 1.

13. Pin strand 8 from right to left diagonally over 7 strands. Work 7 Clove Hitches over strand 8. Pin same strand 8 left to right diagonally over 7 strands. Work 7 Clove Hitches over strand 8.

14. Alternate right and left Clove Hitch groups of 8 all around.

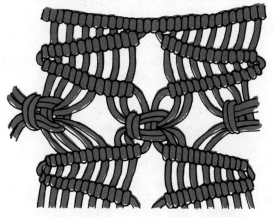

15. Taking 4 strands from each of 2 groups of 8. Tie 8 strand Square Knots all around (2 left and 2 right strands over center 4 Knot Bearer Strands).

16. Work alternate left and right Diagonal Clove Hitches as before.

17. * String a Magenta bead on strand 8 from 1 group and strand 1 from next group; tie a 6 strand Square Knot under bead (strands 6 & 7 from 1 group and strands 2 & 3 from next group over Knot Bearer strands 8 & 1). Skip strands 4 & 5. Repeat from * all around.

18. Thread 1 Magenta, 1 Rose, 1 Pink bead on all 4 & 5 strands. Tie a 6 strand Square Knot as before under Pink bead of each group using strands 4 and 5 as Knot Bearers.

19. Using the same strand as in Magenta bead round tie 6 strand Square Knots 1 inch below Magenta bead.

20. Using same strand as in Step 18 tie 6 strand Square Knots 1 inch below Square Knots.

FRINGE: Divide strands, tie two 8 strand Square Knots (1 left and 1 right over center 6 knot Bearer strands) having the 2 Square Knots 4 inches below last Square Knot.

Trim fringe evenly 9 inches below last Square Knots.

Work Knot Bearer ends under several Clove Hitches to conceal ends on 2nd and 3rd Knot Bearer rounds.

Use top Knot Bearers to adjust neck size.

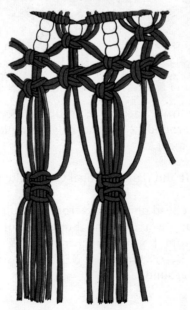

VEST

This macramé vest (given in 1 size) is designed to fit Misses' Sizes 8-14. The original was made from "Aunt Lydia's" Heavy Rug Yarn in a bright color, trimmed with plastic beads. Vest may be worn with pants.

MATERIALS NEEDED:

6 (70 yd.) skeins of Heavy Rug Yarn (75% Rayon, 25% Cotton); 170 plastic barrel beads in a contrasting color; 5/8 yd. of muslin on which to enlarge design from graph; T-Pins or other sturdy pins; scissors; rubber bands; 20" X 22" work board; pencil; No. 0 Steel Crochet Hook; matching heavy duty sewing thread; 5/8" bone ring; darning needle.

DIRECTIONS:

Enlarge graph and draw actual size pattern pieces for Back, Left and Right Fronts on muslin; mark letters, outer and inner lines same as on graph. *Do not cut out pattern pieces.*

Charts for Fronts and Back are given. The symbols used in the Charts indicate the different knots and their placement; follow them carefully.

REVERSE LARK'S HEAD = U
SQUARE KNOT = 2
the numbers inside squares indicate the number of strands to be used for each Square Knot.
HORIZONTAL CLOVE HITCH = ⬤
(Point end of symbol indicates direction for knotting).
DIAGONAL CLOVE HITCH (Left to Right) ⬤
DIAGONAL CLOVE HITCH (Right to Left) ⬤

VEST GRAPH

RIGHT FRONT
1 ☐ = 1 inch

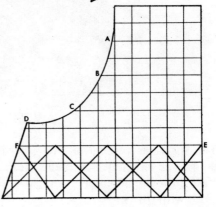

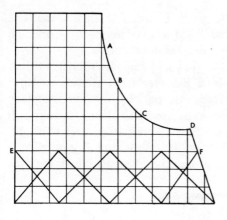

LEFT FRONT

BACK

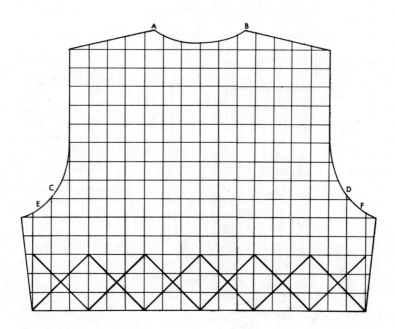

LEFT FRONT: Pin muslin to work board. Cut an 8" length of yarn (Knot Bearer). Make Overhand knots (see pg. 13) on each end 5" apart; pin Knot Bearer along shoulder line.

Cut fourteen (3-½ yd.) lengths of yarn; fold each length in half and with loop end under Knot Bearer, fasten strands to Knot Bearer with Reverse Lark's Heads (see pg. 11). Wind ends of each of the 28 strands into small wads (see pg.10) and fasten with rubber bands. Work each row of Left Front from Left to Right. Separate strands into 1 group of 4 strands and 3 groups of 8 strands each. Pin groups along shoulder line as illustrated (see Detail 1).

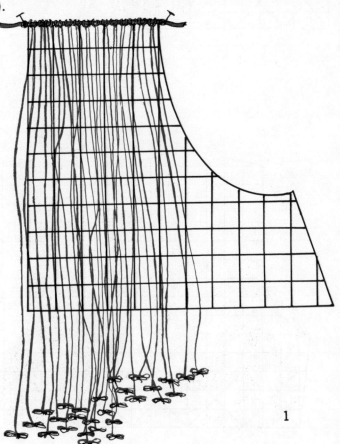

1

Row 1: Starting 1" below Lark's Heads and following Chart, Square Knot one group with 4 strands (see pg. 26) and 3 groups with 8 strands (using 2 strands instead of 1 as in 4-strand group). (Detail 2)

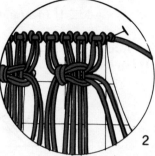

Row 2: Add two (3-½ yd.) strands at Armhole Edge (see A on Chart) as follows: slip cut ends of both strands under and over last 2 strands of last Square Knot of previous row; pull yarn through until all 4 ends are even (see Detail 3); pin loose end of strands in place at Armhole Edge. Following Chart, work 1 group with 8 strands using all 4 strands of first group and 4 strands of next group. Make 3 more (8 strand) groups, always dividing 8 strands of a group in center, using 4 strands of last and 4 strands of next group of previous row. The last group of 8 strands includes the 4 added strands. (See Detail 4). This will form alternating Square Knot group design used in this pattern. Space rows of alternating Square Knot groups 1" apart using lines on muslin pattern as a guide.

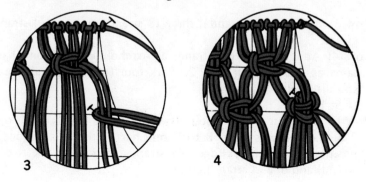

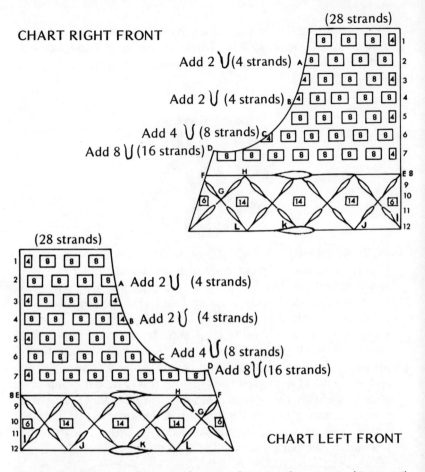

CHART RIGHT FRONT

(28 strands)

Add 2 ∪ (4 strands)

Add 2 ∪ (4 strands)

Add 4 ∪ (8 strands)

Add 8 ∪ (16 strands)

(28 strands)

Add 2 ∪ (4 strands)

Add 2 ∪ (4 strands)

Add 4 ∪ (8 strands)

Add 8 ∪ (16 strands)

CHART LEFT FRONT

Row 3: Work one (4 strand); three (8 strand) and one (4 strand) group.

Row 4: Add two (3 yd.) strands at Armhole Edge (B on Chart) same as described in Row 2. Work four (8 strand) and one (4 strand) group.

Row 5: Follow Chart.

Row 6: Add four (2-¾yd.) strands with Reverse Lark's Heads over 2 outside strands from B to C on Chart; pin added strands in position at Armhole Edge (44 strands in row). Work five (8 strand) and one (4 strand) group.

88

Row 7: Pin outside strand of Armhole Edge in position along curve to end of Armhole on muslin pattern as a Knot Bearer. Add eight (2-½ yd.) strands with Reverse Lark's Heads (C to D on Chart). There will be 60 strands in row; work one (4 strand) and seven (8 strand) groups.

Row 8: Pin a (1 yd.) length of yarn (to be used as a Knot Bearer) for Horizontal Clove Hitch Bar across front over strands of yarn from E to F on Chart, 1" below last Square Knot row. Clove Hitch (see pg. 16) across row using all strands; fasten yarn ends of Knot Bearer securely.

Row 9: Work 1 row of Left to Right Diagonal Clove Hitch (see pg. 20), place and pin first strand of yarn (E on Chart) diagonally down to G (see Detail 5). Use 7 strands for Clove Hitching; pick up 16th strand at (H on Chart); place and pin this diagonally down to G; complete 1 row Right to Left Diagonal Clove Hitch with remaining 7 strands. Clove Hitch next 32 strands in same manner. Add two (2 yd.) strands of yarn (as described in Row 2) at Side Edge below F and complete Right to Left Clove Hitch.

Row 10: Skip first strand at front edge, Square Knot one (6 strand), four (14 strands) and one (6 strand) group (see Chart). For 6 use 2 strands for center and 2 strands taken together for the 2 outside strands. For 14 use 8 strands for center and 3 strands taken together for 2 outside strands. (Detail 6)

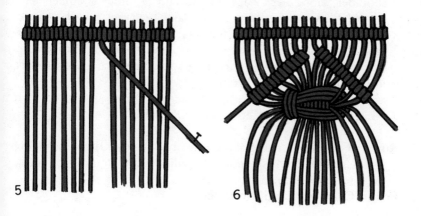

5   6

Row 11: Place and pin 16th strand of first group diagonally to I on Chart crossing 1st strand at G, complete Right to Left Diagonal Clove Hitch; work alternating Left to Right and Right to Left Clove Hitch Bars across row. To join the Diagonal Clove Hitch Bars, knot the 2 center strands at J, K and L.

Row 12: Work another Horizontal Clove Hitch Bar as described in Row 8. (Detail 7)

RIGHT FRONT: Work in reverse of Left Front.

BACK: Cut a 20" length of yarn (Knot Bearer). Make Overhand knots on each end 15" apart. Pin muslin to board and pin Knot Bearer along top of back from beginning to end of one shoulder, along neck edge and to end of other shoulder. Cut forty (3-½ yd.) lengths of yarn. Make 12 Reverse Lark's Heads along each shoulder and 16 along Neck Edge. The number of rows on Back and Fronts do not correspond as Fronts are worked on the *bias* (see photograph). Separate Lark's Heads into groups same as on Front.

(ONLY HALF OF BACK IS GIVEN ON CHART).

Row 1: Following Chart Square Knot two (8 strand) groups taking last 4 strands from shoulder and adjoining 4 strands from neck edge for each group.

Follow Chart from 2nd Row to end.

CHART BACK (½ shown)

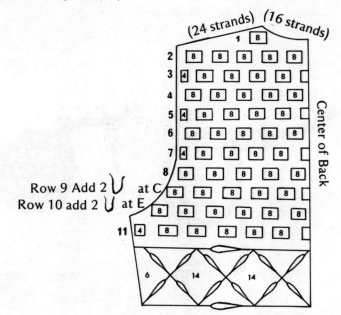

(24 strands) (16 strands)

Center of Back

Row 9 Add 2 ∪ at C
Row 10 add 2 ∪ at E

FINISHING VEST—BLOCKING: Using Muslin Pattern Pieces as a guide, pin each section (wrong side up) to pattern pieces (placed on a padded surface). Cover with a damp cloth; steam (do not press) with hot iron, remove when dry.

JOINING SECTIONS: With right sides out and using matching sewing thread, join sections with invisible stitches along shoulders and underarms.

BEADED FRINGE: Using crochet hook insert each 4 strands of yarn through a bead. Push each bead as close as possible to Clove Hitch Bar at bottom of Vest.

Following photograph, insert 4 strands (two from each 4-strand fringe taken together) through 2 beads. Push beads up to 1-½" below first row of beads.

At beginning and end make 2 fringes of 6 strands.

Trim fringe evenly to measure about 17" from Clove Hitch Bar.

BUTTON: Using 1 strand of rug yarn, cover bone ring with buttonhole stitches (see Detail 8). Push stitches as close together as possible. Fill in center opening by stitching across from one side to opposite side having stitches cross each other (see Detail 9). Stitch button to bottom of Left Front and make a button loop (buttonhole stitches worked over 2 strands of yarn.

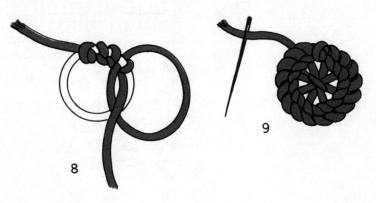

8

9

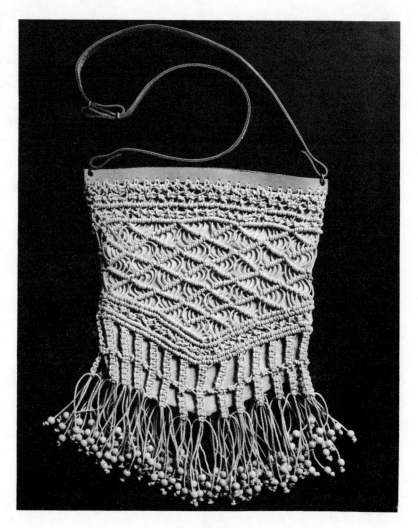

SLING BAG

This bag is exceptionally strong and can hold quite a lot even though its appearance is pleasantly dressy. The firm leather top keeps it in shape and the Velcro closing assures safe carrying of your valuables.

MATERIALS:

2 balls of Seine Cord, two 12" strips of thick, firm leather for top
of bag (width can vary according to your taste—ours is ¾" wide) one
¹⁄₁₆" and one ⅛" Hole Punches, hammer, 112 small wooden
beads, 2 pieces 14" X 14" lining fabric or leather, 2 pieces (12"
long) Velcro for closing, 1 spool matching Carpet Thread to sew
lining to bag, 15" X 15" muslin and Work Board, scissors, crochet
hook, T-Pins, scotch tape and a needle.

DIRECTIONS:

1. Punch 25 holes (using ¹⁄₁₆" punch) evenly spaced across
   lower edge of each leather strip (¼" in from bottom edge).
   Punch holes for attaching handles (using ⅛" punch) where
   indicated on Detail 1.

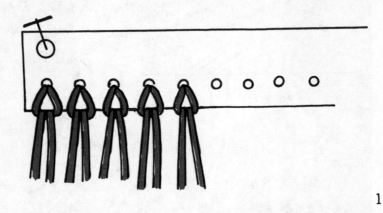

1

2. Cut fifty 3 yard strands of Seine Cord. Make 25 Reverse Lark's
   Heads on each leather strip (1 in each of the ¹⁄₁₆" holes). (Detail
   1) This gives you 50 strands in each strip. Enlarge and draw
   chart on muslin. Pin or tape muslin to Work Board. Pin leather
   strip in position on muslin covered Work Board. From now on
   use this muslin chart as a guide for positioning knots, adding
   Knot Bearers and for angles of Knot Bearers.

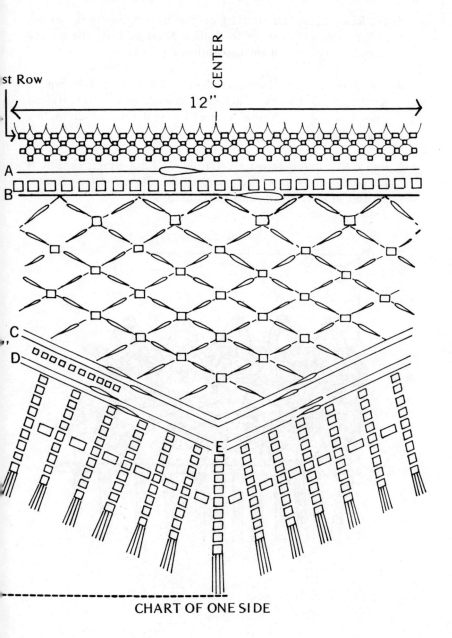

st Row

CENTER

12"

A

B

C

D

E

CHART OF ONE SIDE

95

3. 1st Row—Leave 1st strand free. Square Knot strands (see pg. 25) 2 and 3. Continue to Square Knot each of the next 2 strands to the end of the row following Chart.

4. 2nd Row—Square Knot strands 1 and 2. Continue to Square Knot each of the next 2 strands to the end of this row. Repeat rows 1 and 2 once more. You will have 4 rows of alternating Square Knots.

5. Pin a 14" strand across all strands for Knot Bearer on line A for Horizontal Clove Hitch (see pg.16). Clove Hitch all strands starting at left and working to right edge.

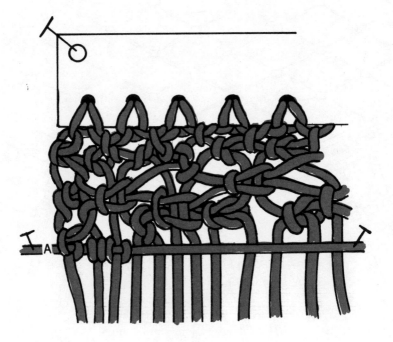

6. Make a row of Square Knots with crossed strands as shown. First Square Knot is made with strands 1 and 3; 2nd Square Knot is made with strands 2 and 4, etc. across the row (Detail 2). Finish row in this manner.

7. Pin a 14" strand across all strands for Knot Bearer on line B. Clove Hitch all strands using strand 1, then 3, then 2, then 4, etc. This gives you the crossed lines below the Square Knot row.

8. Pin strand 6 diagonally from right to left (following lines on muslin). Clove Hitch strands 1-5 on Knot Bearer (strand 6). Pin strand 7 from left to right (following lines on muslin). Clove Hitch strands 8-12 on Knot Bearer (strand 7). Strands 18 and 19 will be the next Knot Bearers. Continue to work this pattern where shown in chart to line C.

9. Pin a 16" long strand along line C and Clove Hitch the left half of strands left to right and the right half of strands from right to left (Detail 3). Add a 2nd 16" long strand on line C and make a 2nd row of Clove Hitching close to the first.

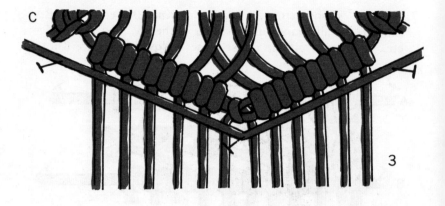

C

3

10. Repeat the crossing and Square Knot procedure in Steps 6 and 7.

11. Pin a 16" long strand along line D and Clove Hitch same as for C. Cut two 1 yard strands and attach with Reverse Lark's Heads to Knot Bearer at point E on Chart.

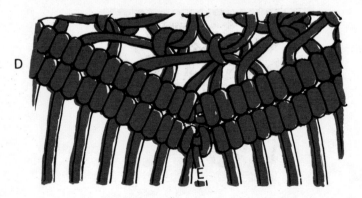

D

E

12. Separate strands into groups of 4, leaving 1 strand free at each side. Make 13 four-knot Square Knot Sennits (see pg.53). Using 1st and 4th strands from each Sennit, Square Knot them to join Sennits as shown.

13. Going back to the original groupings of 4's, continue each Sennit for another 5 Square Knots.

14. String a bead on each strand. Hold in place with an Overhand Knot 4" from end of Sennit. Trim off excess.

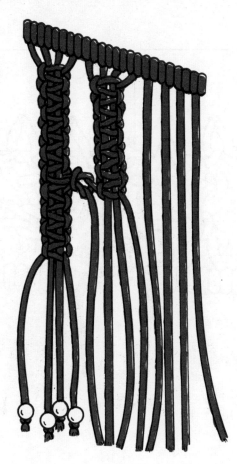

15. Work back in same manner.

16. Join front and back by Square Knotting (adding a folded strand (making 2 working strands) in the top Square Knot at each side and Square Knot the sides together as illustrated. Use a crochet hook to pull the new ends through knots to join as illustrated. When you reach line D, pick up the single strands left on front and back and make the same Sennits you made in steps 12, 13 and 14.

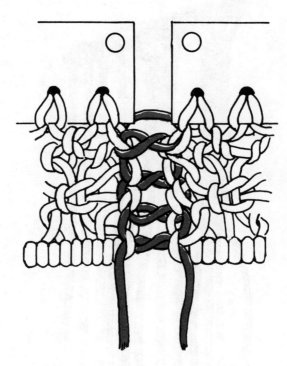

BASIC LINING FOR BAGS AND TOTES

MATERIALS:
2 pieces lining fabric or leather slightly larger than size of bag, 2 pieces of Velcro the width of top of bag (this is optional), 2 pieces of 1″ wide stiff belting, thread to match lining fabric, carpet thread to match, needles, paper to make pattern, pencil. A purchased leather handle was used on the Sling Bag.

DIRECTIONS:
1. Place finished Macramé bag on paper. Draw a line around edges of bag. This will give you the approximate size and shape for lining. Remove bag. Straighten lines and balance sides. Cut 2 pieces of lining ¼″ larger on sides and bottom. Add ¾″ more at top edge.

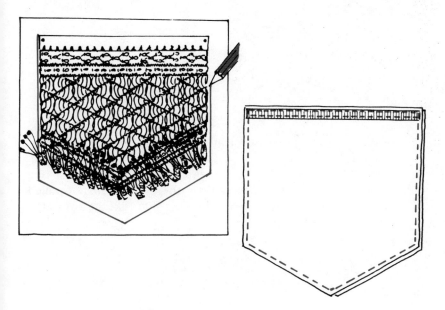

2. Right sides of fabric facing, sew ½″ seams on sides and bottom. Cut 2 strips of stiff belt backing the width of top of lining. Stitch to cut edge of lining on wrong side of fabric. If you

desire a closure for your bag, (we used one on the Sling Bag), cut Velcro the width of the top of the lining. Stitch to right side of fabric 1¼" in from cut edge.

3. Insert lining into bag. Turn under 1" top of lining and sew firmly (using carpet thread) to Knot Bearer or backs of Lark's Heads.

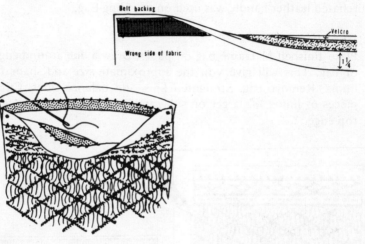

4. When using the purchased leather strap (as on our Sling Bag) you will need pliers to open the rings that attach the handle. Insert ring in hole made on leather strip Knot Bearer. Close ring with pliers. Note that rings used for this purpose are not pulled apart to open but rather twisted to the side (like a gate) so the metal is not weakened.

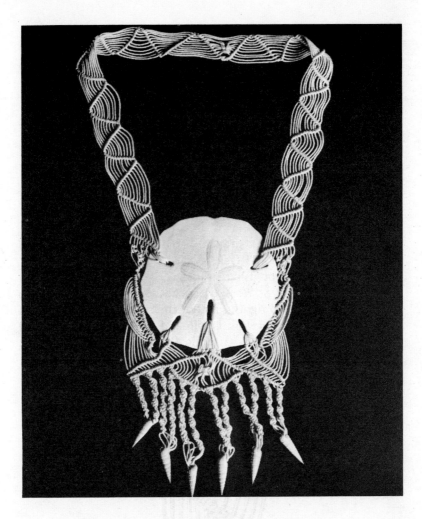

EARTH-WEAR

Here is a necklace where you can incorporate the natural beauties of nature in your Macramé. Since shells are used in this design, the directions given cannot be followed exactly. The size and shape of your shell will determine the number of knots used. No two pieces will ever be exactly the same—lending charm to the necklace.

MATERIALS:

1 Sand Dollar (4″ in diameter); 6 Spiral Shells (1″ long); 1 skein Double Quick Cotton; Sobo glue, Work Board (approx. 9″ X 12″), T-pins, scissors.

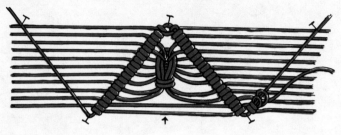

DIRECTIONS:

1. Cut 12 (3½ yard length strands). Pin center of strands to top of Work Board. Bunch and tack 12 back strands to back of Board. Make a Square Knot using strands 3, 4 and 9, 10 over Knot Bearers 5, 6, 7 and 8. Work Diagonal Clove Hitch from right to left and back left to right using the same outside strand as Knot Bearer throughout for 11″. Unpin and work 11″ on other side in same manner ending with the Diagonal Clove Hitching at each side facing toward the center.

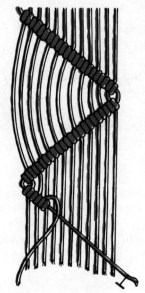

2. Pull 6 strands from each strip through top holes in shell.

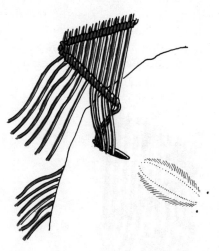

3. Turn shell face down. Pin securely to board. Work a Horizontal Clove Hitch across the 12 strands at each side of back of shell.

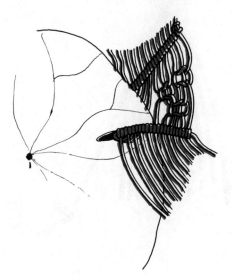

4. Unpin. Turn shell right side up. Pin worked strands securely to board. Make 3 alternating Square Knots where illustrated. Pin same Knot Bearer as before across the remaining 11 strands. Knot Bearer should follow contour of shell. Work a row of Clove Hitch Knots using all strands. Make a 2nd row of Clove Hitch Knots using the new outside strand as Knot Bearer.

5. Pin same 2 Knot Bearers, taken together, to follow the contour of shell. Clove Hitch all strands on Knot Bearer.

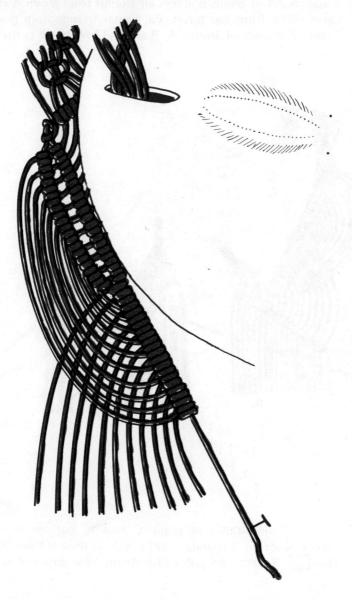

6. Cut 12 strands 48″ long. Lark's Head (See page 11) 3 strands on 2 outside holes (B) and 6 strands on center hole (C) of shell. Pin inside strand of group B across all strands from group A and B, Clove Hitch from top down. Pin center strands from group C across all strands of groups A, B and C. Clove Hitch entire row.

7. Pin 4 middle strands of group C taut to bottom of board. Square Knot the 2 strands to either side of these 4 Knot Bearers (an 8 Square Knot). Pin 13th strand from center of group C

as a Knot Bearer across the 11 middle strands. Clove Hitch.
Balance both sides. You now have 48 strands. Make 12
four-strand Twist Sennits (Sennit # 2 on page 54). Bottom of
Sennits should form a gentle point. Cut off excess material and,
grouping Sennits in two's, glue the 8 strands inside each Spiral
Shell.

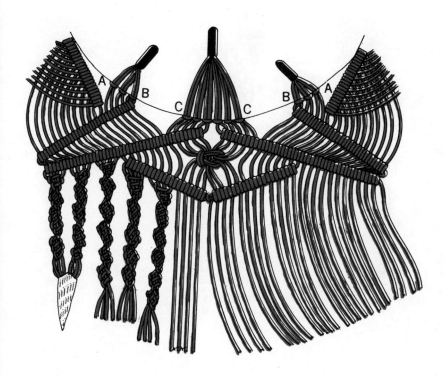

The above directions will necessarily vary with the size shells used. You may find it unnecessary to Clove Hitch where we have indicated. The materials you use will determine the necessary changes in design. That is what makes it so intriguing. No two designs (even made by the same person) are really the same.

PILLOW 15″ × 15″

We used chartreuse and peacock blue "Aunt Lydia's" Heavy Rug Yarn for this macramé pillow. The striped design will fit easily into a modern or traditional home. It is done entirely in Square Knots. Any two contrasting colors to fit your color scheme can be used.

MATERIALS:

2 (70 yd.) skeins of Color A and 3 skeins Color B "Aunt Lydia's" Heavy Rug Yarn, an 18" X 18" piece of muslin on which to mark guide lines for design; 18" X 18" Work Board (corrugated cardboard); scissors, T-Pins or similar sturdy pins; rubber bands; soft pencil; darning needle; matching sewing thread; a 15" X 15" square pillow covered with one of the colors used for macramé.

MARKING MUSLIN:

With a soft pencil draw a 15" X 15" square for outline of macramé on muslin piece, then draw a horizontal line 1" from top line; *another line 1" from last line and another one 2" from last line; repeat from * 3 times, end with another line 1" from last line. Use these as guide lines for Square Knot stripes.

MACRAMÉ DIRECTIONS:

Pin muslin to Work Board. Cut an 18" length yarn Color B for Knot Bearer. Make a knot on each end 15" apart; pin Knot Bearer along top line of marked square on muslin covered Work Board. Cut 30 (3¼ yd.) strands of Color B and 30 (4¼ yd.) strands Color A. Fold strands in half and with loop end under Knot Bearer, fasten strands to Knot Bearer with Reverse Lark's Heads (see page 11). Follow Chart (only ¼ of Pillow top is shown on Chart) for placement of Lark's Heads in Colors A and B. There will be 60 strands of each color in row. Wind ends of strands into small wads and fasten with rubber bands. Separate strands into 15 groups of 8 strands (2 strands A, 4 strands B and 2 strands A) in each group.

Row 1: Following Chart and working from left to right, tie 15 Square Knots (see page 25) with 8 strands (2 strands Color A left and right over 4 center Knot Bearers strands B) forming 8A Square knot groups.

Row 2: Keep strands (Color B) in back of Color A strands. Work with A strands only. Skip first 2 strands, tie 14 Square Knots with 4 strands (see page 25); skip last 2 strands. Square Knots are formed between Square Knots of previous row using 2 strands from one group together with 2 strands of next group (see Chart).

Row 3: Tie 15 Square Knots with Color A.

Row 4: Repeat Row 2.

(CHART FOR ¼ OF PILLOW)

A = Peacock

B = Chartreuse

U = Reverse Lark's Head

4 8 = Square Knot

Numbers inside squares indicate the number of strands to be used for each Square Knot. The letters indicate the color used.

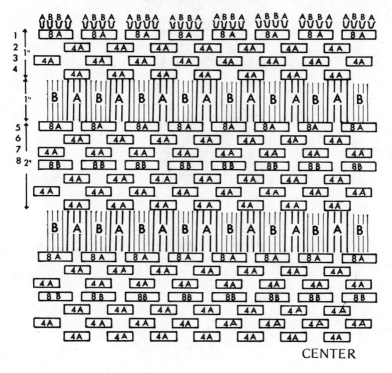

CENTER

Row 5. Repeat Row 1, forming Square Knots along 2nd guide line from top row which is 1" below last row of Knots (see Detail 1).

Rows 6 AND 7: Repeat rows 2 and 3.

Row 8: Tie 15 Square Knots with Color B (2 strands—Color B—left and right over 4 center strands Color A forming 8B Square Knot groups.

Repeat rows (2, 3, 4, 5, 6, 7 and 8) 3 times.

Repeat rows 2 through 6 once more.

Unpin macramé. Trim ends to about 4". Using a darning needle, weave ends of strands through wrong side of macramé (see page 52).

With matching sewing thread, stitch macramé to top of pillow.

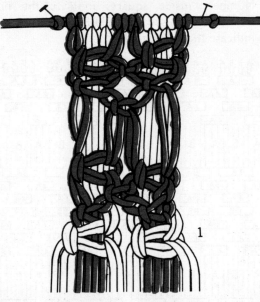

SENNIT—(to be used as cord around Pillow).

Cut 4 (14 yd.) lengths Color B yarn (for left and right side strands)

Cut four 14 yard lengths and two 4½ yard lengths of Color B. Make a Square Knot Sennit (see page 53) long enough to fit around pillow. Stitch Sennit ends together and weave in loose ends, then attach to pillow edge over Macramé.

JUTE PLANT HANGER

JUTE PLANT HANGER

MATERIALS:

1 skein Jute Tone; scotch tape. Work Board; T-pins; plastic ice cream container (1 quart size)

DIRECTIONS:

1. Cut 12 strands each 8 yds. long. Make bobbins of all ends 2" from center.

2. Make a Square Knot (Method 2—Pg. 29) in center of all 12 strands.

3. ¾" from center Square Knot make 12 ☐2 Square Knots to form a circle as illustrated.

4. Group strands in sets of 4. Make 6 Square Knot Sennits (See page 28) 7 knots long.

5. Center Square Knot on bottom of container and scotch tape Sennits to sides of container. Taking 2 strands from 1 group and 2 from the next, make 6 ☐4 Square Knot Sennits 5 knots long, approx. ¾" from Sennit. Roll Sennits and bring Knot Bearers over top of Sennit. Make 1 more Square Knot below Sennit to hold roll in place (See Detail A).

6. Taking 2 strands from 1st group and 2 strands from 2nd group make 6 ☐4 Sennits 15 knots long. Keep in line with Sennits from step 5.

7. 1" from Sennits join 2 Sennits, using 4 strands as Knot Bearers, and Square Knot with 2 strands on left and 2 strands on right over Knot Bearers, 20 Knots.
Make 3 such Sennits as Illustrated.

8. Group all strands neatly at top. Wrap strands 15 times. (See page 14).

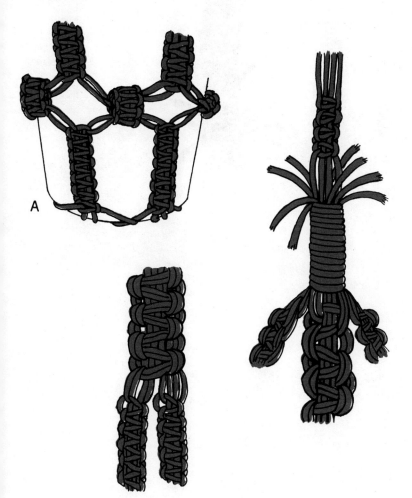

A

9. Make a 4 Square Knot Sennit of 15 Knots. Turn end back and Overhand Knot together with 5 wraps as illustrated. Cut all ends even for fringe.

DOG LEASH

MATERIALS:

60 yards of Seine Cord; metal hook fastener; Work Board (8" X 12" corrugated board); T-pins, rubber bands, scotch tape, scissors; a sturdy darning needle with large eye.

DIRECTIONS:

(Dog leash is started at center of top loop).

1. Cut 6 strands each 10 yds. long and make a knot on each end to prevent ravelling.

2. Fold each strand in half and pin fold-end of each strand to top edge of Work Board. Wind both ends of 6 strands into small wads (See page 10); fasten with rubber bands.

3. Working with 6 strands in front of board, form a 6 strand Square Knot Sennit (1 strand each at right and left side of 4 Knot Bearer strands) 6¼" long. (See page 53 for Square Knot Sennit). Working with the 6 strands in back of Work Board form a 12½" long Sennit. Remove work from board.

4. Fold Sennit in half; join the 2 halves to form top loop with a 12 strand Simple Overhand Knot (See page 13). Divide 12 strands into two 6 strand groups and make an Overhand Knot with each 6-strand

group, then another 12 strand Overhand Knot.

5. Pin work to Work Board again and divide 12 strands into 2 groups of 6 strands each; work a 6 strand Twisting Sennit (see page 54) using 2 strands each at right and left side of 2 Knot Bearer strands (always use the 2 shortest strands as Knot Bearers or part of Knot Bearer strands). Make each Sennit 4" long.

6. Join the 2 Twisting Sennits by working 2 Square Knots (See page 28) with all 12 strands (2 strands each at right and left side of 8 Knot Bearer strands). Make groups of 2 Square Knots 1" below last Square Knot group until 17 (2 Square Knot groups) are completed.

7. Repeat Step 5, but work Sennits 4½" long.

8. Join Sennits with a 12 strand Overhand Knot, then two 6 strand Overhand Knots as described in Step 4. Cut off end of 5 strands 1½" from last 2 knots.

9. End with a 10 Knot Square Knot Sennit, same as described in Step 3 using 6 center strands, starting 1½" below last 2 knots.

10. Insert Sennit through loop end of metal hook fastener, fold it back in half and cut off ends of Sennit 1½" below last Square Knot. Wrap the remaining strand about 12 times tightly around all 17 strands. Thread needle with end of strand; fasten end securely by pushing needle from bottom to top inside wrapped part. (Wrapped Knot See page 14). Cut off all ends.

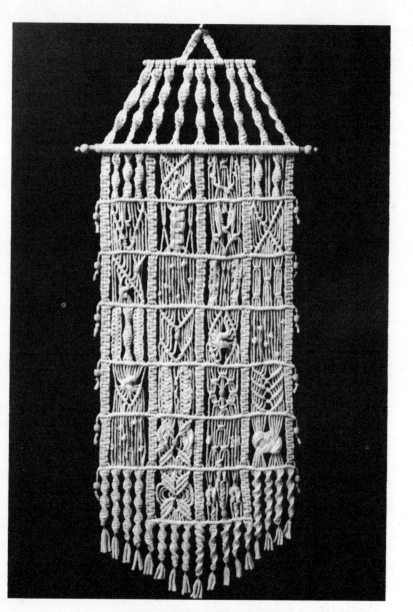

SAMPLER WALL HANGING

SAMPLER WALL HANGING

MATERIALS:

One 8½" dowel (¼" diameter); one 15" dowel (⅜" diameter); 6 skeins "Aunt Lydia's" Heavy Rug Yarn—natural; T-pins, scissors, rubber bands, Work Board (approx. 2' X 4'); 18" X 39" piece of muslin on which to draw guide lines; 72 amber Pony Beads; 12 natural wood Barrel Beads; 2 large round wood beads for ends of dowels; 2 medium round wood beads for ends of dowels; Push pins; crochet hook #0 Steel.

DIRECTIONS:

1. Enlarge graph and draw actual size on muslin. Pin muslin graph to Work Board.

2. Cut 18 ten yard lengths of rug yarn. Fold each length in half and with the loop end, make 18 Lark's Heads on the ¼" diameter dowel. Make small loops of scrap yarn and attach dowel to Work Board with these small loops. Wind ends of each strand into small wads and fasten with rubber bands.

3. Separate strands into groups of 4 each. Work 9 Sennits to line A. We used the Twisting Sennit on page 54, but you may substitute any 4 strand Sennit you want.

4. Place ⅜" dowel to be used as a Knot Bearer on line A—hold in place same as other dowel. Horizontal Clove Hitch 4 strands of first Sennit, add 4 strands with 2 Reverse Lark's Heads, continue along dowel alternating Clove Hitching of 4 strands of Sennit and the 4 strands added by 2 Lark's Heads—end by Clove Hitching strands of 9th Sennit. Adjust strands so they are spaced evenly along dowel (68 strands).

5. Work Sennits of strands (1, 2, 3, 4)—(17, 18, 19, 20)—(33, 34, 35, 36)—(49, 50, 51, 52) and (65, 66, 67, 68) to line B. We used the Square Knot Sennit on page 53. These Sennits will act as frames for your sample squares.

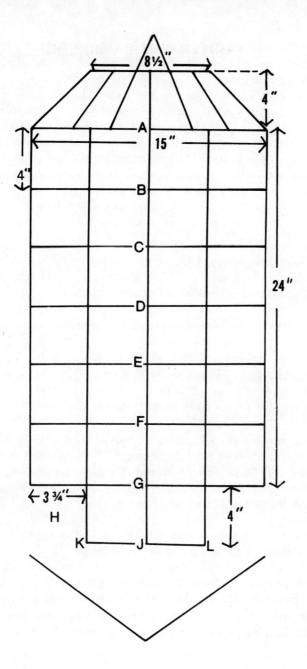

6. Each block of the Wall Hanging is really a sample of a knot or combination of knots. For example, our first row of sampler squares consists of—
Square 1—3 Twisting Sennits (See page 54).
Square 2—A V Clove Hitch (See page 24) for the upper third, a Reverse V (See page 22) for the center section with a Square Knot (See page 25) of the 2 center strands and another V Clove Hitch for bottom section.
Square 3—Seven 2 strand Square Knots form a U plus one 4 strand Square Knot in the center.
Square 4—Single strand—4 strand Twisting Sennit—2 single strands—4 strand Twisting Sennit—and 1 single strand.

To make this truly YOUR Wall Hanging, make up your own samples for each square. This is a pretty way to keep note on your favorite knot combinations and patterns.

7. Pin an 18" Knot Bearer over line B. Clove Hitch across entire piece.

8. Repeat Steps 5, 6 and 7 to line C (Clove Hitch Line).

9. Repeat Step 8 four more times (total of 6 sampler rows).

10. Make four 4 strand Twisting Sennits of strands 1-16—(20 Half Hitches on Sennit 1, 24 on Sennit 2, 28 on Sennit 3 and 32 on Sennit 4). Make four 4 strand Twisting Sennits of strands 52-68—(32 Half Hitches on the first Sennit, 28 on the second, 24 on the 3rd and 20 on the fourth).

11. Make one 4 strand Square Knot Sennit of strands 17-20, one of strands 33-36 and one of strands 49-51—all to line J. Make 2 pattern squares in 2 remaining boxes. Add Knot Bearer and work Horizontal Clove Hitch across from K to L.

12. Make nine 4 strand Twisting Sennits from remaining strands (12 Half Hitches on first Sennit, 16 on second, 20 on third, 24

on fourth, 28 on fifth, 24 on sixth, 20 on seventh, 16 on eighth and 12 on ninth Sennit). String 1 Pony Bead using crochet hook on each 4 strand ending to each Sennit (17 in all). Trim ends 1″ below bead and fluff into a tassel.

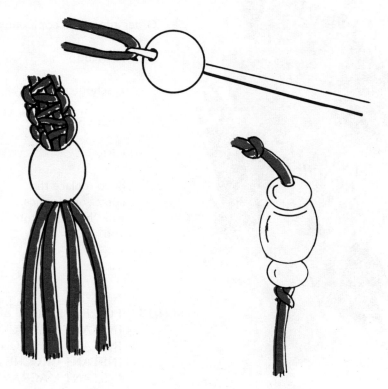

13. Unpin Horizontal Anchor Cords. String 1 Pony Bead, 1 wood Barrel Bead, another Pony Bead on each of the ends. Push beads to ½″ from Clove Hitch. Make an Overhand Knot to hold beads in place. Trim off all but ½″ of end. Fluff into a tassel.

14. Using a thin nail, tack wooden beads to ends of dowel.

EXTRA   EXTRA   EXTRA   EXTRA

4 INSTANT BOOKS

Order additional copies now.

for   A friend

A school

Your church

Gifts

or to replace the
copy your friends
will "borrow" from
you.

SEND $1. FOR EACH COPY of
INSTANT SEWING
INSTANT FASHION
INSTANT CROCHET
INSTANT MACRAMÉ

to
INSTANT BOOKS
Box 155, Old Chelsea Station
New York, N.Y., 10011

INSTANT BOOKS
60 Front Street
Toronto 1, Ontario
Canada

Please add 25¢ for postage and handling for each book.